the Book of Courtly Love

the Book of Courtly Love

MEDIEVAL STORIES AND SONGS

EDITED BY ROBERT YAGLEY

BARNES
&NOBLE
BOOKS
NEW YORK

ACKNOWLEDGMENTS

Paul Blackburn's translations of Raimon Jordan's "I see the clear weather darken," Jaufré Rudel's "When, from the spring, the stream," Guillem IX's "Song seizes me . . . ," Bertran de Born's "I want to make a half-a-sirventes . . . ," and Arnaut de Mareuil's "The wind is fair" from *Proensa: An Anthology of Troubadour Poetry*. Copyright © 1978 by Joan Blackburn. Reprinted with the permission of Regents of the University of California.

Meg Bogin's translations of the Countess of Dia's "I thrive on youth and joy" and "Fine joy brings me great happiness," Alamanda's and Giraut de Bornelh's "Tenzon," and Isabella's and Elias Cairel's "Tenzon" from *The Women Troubadours* (New York, N.Y.: W.W. Norton & Company, 1980). Reprinted with the permission of Magda Bogin.

Frederick Goldin's translations of Cercamon's "When the sweet breeze turns bitter," Bernart de Ventadorn's "Lords, counsel me now," Giraut de Bornelh's "When the ice and the cold and the snow," Gace Brulé's "The little birds of my country," Colin Muset's "Would you like to hear the *muse* of Muset?" from *Lyrics of the Troubadours & Trouvères* (Garden City, N.Y.: Anchor Press/Doubleday, 1973). Copyright © 1973 by Frederick Goldin. His translations of Heinrich von Veldeke's "In April when the flowers spring," Friedrich von Hausen's "I think sometimes about," Heinrich von Morungen's "It has gone with me as with a child," Walther von der Vogelweide's "Under the lime tree" from *German and Italian Lyrics of the Middle Ages* (Garden City, N.Y.: Anchor Press/Doubleday, 1973). Copyright © 1973 by Frederick Goldin. Reprinted with the permission of Frederick Goldin.

Geoffrey O'Brien's translation of Bernart de Ventadorn's "When I see the lark move" originally appeared in *Res Gestae*, edited by Peter Fusco. Reprinted with the permission of Geoffrey O'Brien.

J. J. Parry's translation of "The Rules of Courtly Love" from *The Art of Courtly Love* by Andreas Capellanus. Copyright © 1941 by Columbia University Press. Reprinted with the permission of the publisher.

Contents

Origins of the Courtly Love Lyric

HE STORIES AND SONGS of the courtly love tradition have been retold so often and have influenced so many generations that they have come to occupy a large portion of the medieval landscape. To many readers, the legends about King Arthur and poems of the troubadours lend the Middle Ages its aura of shimmering spectacle. Does it matter what the historical importance of the troubadour was, when the poetry of courtly romance that has survived continues to bloom and shed blossoms over the castle ruins of its time? Well, yes, for where the courtly love tradition actually flourished it imparts to the dry readings of history a sense of mystery, and even a touch of the marvelous.

Though obscured by time, it is possible to recognize the origins of the courtly love lyric in both the *chanson de geste* (song of fact) and the sensuality of Islamic song.

The *chanson de geste*, which flourished just after A.D. 1000, was sung by wandering minstrels and clerks to draw pilgrims to the shrines where the epic heroes were buried. The material for these songs was gathered from the recorded histories of saints and heroes in the monasteries and churches where their relics were enshrined. Though the minstrels heavily embroidered on the original histories, the songs were taken as fact by a naive laity. The *chanson's* most popular subject was Charlemagne and his circle, and its most notable composition, the *Chanson de Roland*, was an immense rewriting of one of his failed military expeditions. However historically incorrect the *chansons* were, what is significant to note here is that they championed the virtues of chivalry and gallantry.

If the courage portrayed in the *chanson de geste* foreshadowed the valor evident in the practice of courtly love, the influence of the Moslem courts imbued troubadour poetry with a physicality much at odds with the abstract tendencies of Western thought. When the Moslem rulers were driven out of Aragon, the northern region of Spain, their people still inhabited the land and lived side by side with Christians. In the late eleventh century, Moslem culture was allowed to continue unhindered by the new ruling families from the West. Both the lute and viol, two favorite instruments of the troubadour, originated in the East and were introduced into Europe by the Moors. The verse forms of Hispano-Arabic love poetry, which was often accompanied by musical instruments, also predate the troubabours by at least a century.

Though some scholars assert the Latin origin of the courtly love lyric, there are enough similarities to the Arabic song to acknowledge it as the precursor of the troubadour's art. Besides those aspects mentioned above, the rhythms of the troubadour lyrics in the *aube* (dawn song) or *ballad* had close affinities to the Andalusian *zajal*, a lyrical form popular among both Christian and Moslem poets. Also there was the spiritual influence of Sufi poetry, which, although strongest in Persia, had its practitioners in Moslem Spain. Similar to the troubadour's *gai sçavoir* (gay science) was the Sufi belief that an understanding of profane love is essential to grasp the truth of spiritual love.

Both the *chanson de geste* and the Hispano-Arabic culture were healthy and active in the early twelfth century, and they would have had a considerable influence on the art and life of Guillem IX, Count of Poitiers and Orange, who is generally recognized as the first troubadour. Born in 1071, he would have been familiar with both of these forerunners of the courtly love lyric. He grew up in the region south of the Loire where the *chansons* were widely known. Later, he would marry the Countess of Aragon, whose court and country were laden with Moslem influences. When he was called to the First Crusade, he reluctantly joined, but his part in the successful adventure was unremarkable, except for its effect of liberating him from the conventions of his homeland. Not until his return from the East is there any record of the compositions that would come to be considered the beginning of the courtly love tradition.

Poitiers in the twelfth century was a powerful and wealthy domain that wielded considerable sway over European politics. The court of Poitiers attracted a number of counts and ladies who, anxious for the company of its lord, developed a first-hand knowledge of the new *chanson*, or song of the court. From Guillem IX's court spread the art of the courtly lyric, which would find its further expression in the troubadours Cercamon and Marcabru, who found patronage under Guillem IX's son, Guillem X. In 1121, Guillem X married Anor, the daughter of his father's mistress. A year later, Anor gave birth to Eleanor of Aquitaine, who during her marriage to Henry II of England started her "courts of love" at her residence in Poitiers. It was there in 1171 that her daughter, Marie de Champagne, commissioned Andreas Capellanus to write his "Art of Courtly Love," and later, Chrétien de Troyes to write "Lancelot, Knight of the Cart" and other narrative poems.

The troubadour poets that flourished in the Provençe region of France composed their work in the *langue d'oc*, while their companions to the north were known as *trouvères* and composed in the *langue d'oïl*. (Modern French is descended from the latter.) But in the beginning of the thirteenth century, the epoch of the troubadour was drawing to a close. The Albigensian Crusade against the southern feudal domains of France, which the Church viewed as heretical for their disregard of papal authority, devastated the culture and language of the troubadours. With the success of the papal armies, some of the Provençal poets were exiled to Germany and Italy, where their lyrics would influence the verse of the German minne-singers, and, later, the Italian poets, including such notables as Guido Cavalcanti and Dante Alighieri. At this juncture with Dante, in the early fourteenth century, the distinction between the end of the Middle Ages and the beginnings of the Renaissance becomes obscured. Yet the spirit of romance, carried over from the Middle Ages by the Renaissance, continued to nourish the arts of the Romantic and Pre-Raphaelite periods as well as the works of such twentieth-century poets as Ezra Pound and Paul Blackburn.

— ROBERT YAGLEY

1997

Suggested Further Reading

Barber, Richard, ed. *The Arthurian Legends: An Illustrated Anthology* (New York: Barnes & Noble Books, 1993).

Gilbert, Dorothy, trans. *Chrétien de Troyes's Erec and Enide* (Berkeley: University of California Press, 1992).

Hanning, Robert & Ferrante, Joan, trans. *The Lais of Marie de France* (Grand Rapids, MI: Baker Books, 1995).

Marks, Claude. *Pilgrims, Heretics, and Lovers: A Medieval Journey* (New York: Macmillan, 1975).

Seward, Desmond. *Eleanor of Aquitaine: The Mother Queen* (New York: Barnes & Noble Books, 1993).

all for love

COURTLY LOVE DELIGHTED in obstacles. Never the straight and narrow, its realm encompassed the kingdoms, families, statuses, and physical prowess and beauty of the lovers who subscribed to its laws. To be among its participants was no small thing. A show of fin' amours (fine love) was a sure sign the lover was familiar with the ways of nobility.

Of Love, in honor of his Mistress Becchina

Whatever good is naturally done
   Is born of Love as fruit is born of flower:
   By Love all good is brought to its full power:
Yea, Love does more than this; for he finds none
So coarse but from his touch some grace is won,
   And the poor wretch is altered in an hour.
   So let it be decreed that Death devour
The beast who says that Love's a thing to shun.
A man's just worth the good that he can hold,
   And where no love is found, no good is there;
      On that there's nothing that I would not stake
So now, my Sonnet, go as you are told
      To lovers and their sweethearts everywhere,
         And say I made you for Becchina's sake.

CECCO ANGIOLIERI, DA SIENA
Translated from Italian by Dante Gabriel Rossetti

"When the sweet breeze turns bitter"

When the sweet breeze turns bitter
and the leaf falls down from the branch
and the birds change their language,
I, here, sigh, and sing
of Love, who holds me bound and captured,
Love, whom I never have had in my power.

I am weary, for I have won nothing from love
but toil and torture,
for nothing is so hard to get
as the thing I desire;
and nothing fills me with such longing
as the thing I cannot have.

I rejoice in a jewel
so precious that I never loved another thing so much;
when I am with her I am struck so dumb,
I cannot tell her my desire,
and when I go away from her I think
I lose my mind completely, and everything I know.

The most beautiful lady a man ever saw
is not worth a glove next to *her*;
when the whole world grows dark,
where she is—see, there is light.
God let me live long enough to have her,
or see her going to bed.

I start, I burn, I tremble, all over,
sleeping and waking, for love of her.
I am so afraid of dying,
I dare not think of asking her;
however, I shall serve her two years or three,
and then, maybe, she will know the truth.

I neither die, nor live, nor get well,
I do not feel my suffering, and yet it is great suffering,
because I cannot tell the future of her love,
whether I shall have it, or when,
for in her is all the pity,
which can raise me up, or make me fall.

I am pleased when she maddens me,
when she makes me stand with my mouth open, staring;
I am pleased when she laughs at me,
or makes a fool of me right to my face or behind my
   back,
for after this bad time the good will come,
very quickly, if such is her pleasure.

If she does not want me, I would have liked to die
that day, when she took me as her servant;
oh lord, how gently she slew me
when she showed me the look of her love,
and locked me in such an enclosure,
I never want to see another.

I am full of worries and yet I enjoy it,
for if I fear my lady and court her,
I will be false or true, it all depends on her,
faithful or full of tricks,
a vulgar or a courtly man,
full of torment or at my ease.

It may please some and annoy others,
but she can retain me, if that's what she wants.

Cercamon says: a man will hardly belong in court
if he despairs of love.

CERCAMON

Translated from Provençal by Frederick Goldin

the BiRth of tRistan

IN THE LAND OF PARMENIE, an ambitious, bold, and freehanded knight named Rivalin grew up from boyhood practicing the knightly skills of arms and chivalry in the domain of his lord, Duke Morgan. Now three years after gaining knighthood, Rivalin raised an army and marched into his lord's lands, righteously claiming his lord's neglect of leadership. And as many knights agreed with him, Rivalin soon was able to lay siege to Morgan's castles, a good many of which he captured. On his side, Morgan gathered his forces and counter-attacked with much efficiency; so that many deeds of knighthood were witnessed on both sides. But the surmounting battles took a heavy toll upon the armies, so that after some debating, they thought to establish a truce of one year.

Rivalin returned home with his knights and distributed his spoils freely, but although he was glad with his spoils, he still longed for further honor. So with twelve companions, he set out from his lands to find adventure at the court of the young King Mark, the King of Cornwall, whose name he had heard linked to so many valiant deeds. In his absence, Rivalin left his lands in the care of his marshal, Rual, whom men called the Faith-keeper.

Once in the Cornish lands, the court of King Mark at Tintagel lived up to many of Rivalin's expectations; the knights and ladies clad themselves in fine robes, King Mark received them courteously, and his men were treated by his court with great respect and honor. Now every month of May, King Mark held a high feast wherein all the knights and their ladies gathered to participate in chivalric sports, dancing, and much mirth-making. Tents were pitched in the meadows of Tintagel, flowers spotted the grass, birds sang in the thickets, the tree boughs swayed lightly in the spring winds, and the ladies were fair in both their figures and speech. In the late afternoon, the knightly jousts commenced with their audience lodged in brightly colored pavilions of silk. Then after the games came the feast and then more dancing. Thus they passed the entire day making much fun and gallantry.

Yet of all the wondrous maidens there that day, none fared to stir Rivalin's heart as did the king's sister, Blanchefleur. And of all the valiant young men there enjoying King Mark's feast, none attracted Blanchefleur's flights of fancy as much as did this courageous foreigner, Prince Rivalin. Though neither made their desires known, they both knew who they favored above all others.

It then perchanced that the young prince espied Blanchefleur alone beside the forest's edge.

"God keep thee, sweet lady."

"Good mercy," said the maiden, "God give thee good fortune . . . though I think I have something against thee."

"Ah, how could I hurt thee."

To which she replied, "Thou hast caused me to sorrow for someone very close."

Then the knight panicked thinking he had in jousting overthrown or wounded a kinsman or dear friend of hers. But the maiden was thinking of her own heart. And as the young knight thought upon her words, how she looked and her voice, love and sorrow was kindled in his heart too. Though no word passed between them, their eyes told each other's tale, so that as the hours passed their knowledge of the other's love widened in both their hearts and minds.

As the days of the feast winded down with the guests gradually departing for their homelands, word came to King Mark that one of his foes had entered his lands and was laying great waste to it. Then Mark gathered a large army and rode against him. A great battle ensued and such was the slaughter on both sides that any man who escaped with his life could be called most fortunate. The forces of King Mark finally carried the day, but the unfortunate Rivalin was brought back to Tintagel with a spear wound in his side.

At first, rumor went about the court that he was slain, and a great lamentation was made by many knights, but particularly by Blanchefleur who wept, tore her hair, and was ready to die for grief. She must, she thought to herself, see the young knight once more, even if he were already dead. So she sent for her mistress of the court and ordered her to set things up that she might make her visit to him alone.

Her mistress of the court, being quite clever, dressed the maiden in the guise of a wise woman skilled in herbs and then brought her, unbeknownst to all, to the bedside of the dying knight. Seeing him lie in bed seemingly lifeless and pale, she fell down swooning. Then she raised him in her arms and kissed him over and over again, till her kisses brought him back to life and her love gave him strength to live.

So Rivalin recovered; but the two still kept their love secret, for they had little hope that Mark would give his sister to a foreigner, and none but her mistress of the court knew of their affair or deemed how often they in secret met.

But news came to Rivalin that his foe, Duke Morgan, had broken their truce and marched into his kingdom. Rual, the Faith-keeper, held back the enemy forces, but prayed that his lord would return in all haste and defend his lands. So Rivalin went to tell Blanchefleur the troubling news, and she fell to weeping piteously.

"O such sad tidings," she cried. "What am I going to do here alone? My grief for loss of thee will be so grave that my brother, Mark, will know I hath given my love without his will. Then from me will he take my lands, casting me out to die."

"What then?" cried Rivalin. "Should I forfeit my lands and money to my enemies? Or wilt thou leave with me now, by night, to my lands? I will do whatever pleaseth thee best."

"I will come with thee," said Blanchefleur. So that evening, while Rivalin went to say good-bye to King Mark, the princess disguised herself and, under the cover of night, stole out of the castle and down to Rivalin's ship leaving for Parmenie.

But when they came to Rivalin's country they found that Morgan had gathered together a vast army, and all the land trembled at the thought of him. Yet before Rivalin collected his forces, in the presence of all his nobles, and with the counsel of Rual, Prince Rivalin wedded Blanchefleur, so that for a few days they were happy in each other's love.

Soon his army was raised and Rivalin led them forth into battle. The war was fierce and awful, till at last the entire armies of both met on one field, then were many valiant knights slain and cut down, and, alas! Rivalin was among them.

When they brought the news to Blanchefleur, she spoke no word and shed no tear, but for four days she lay without speaking, and on the fourth day she gave birth to a fine baby boy, and then died.

Now when Rual, the Faith-keeper, saw that both his lord and lady were dead he knew he must need make peace with Morgan. Yet he feared that Morgan should harm the young baby and rightful heir of the land, so he had it claimed abroad that the baby had died with its mother, and then secretly he brought the child to his wife, and then told all that she had borne him another son.

Rivalin and Blanchefleur were then buried in one grave, and all thought that their child lay with them; but the babe was safe in Rual's care, and he named him *Tristan*, and brought him up as his own son.

from TRISTAN AND ISOLT by Gottfried von Strassburg
Translated from German by Jessie Weston, adapted by the editor

from **"I see the clear weather darken"**

All my thought's on Love, I
give my deed in his service.
It redounds much to my credit
and I should thank God for it,
for I've been able to discern
the best the world has got.
Any one of you would turn
gladhearted to be welcomed by
            her
      where my thought
      turns & returns.

I am lover & I'll be hers
as long as I've life at all.
And don't think I'll fall
short before she advances me.
I supplicate toward where she lives,
pray, adore and bend with faithful heart
and turn my eyes often toward that place.
            I love her well.

Damn!
I am
            in such distress
            to see that place
            tower and wall!
at least to reassure my heart
that they still stand,
for messenger I've none but
my own heart in warrant.

And if I comfort myself at all
        it's with the thought
        that she'll not
hear nor understand against me aught,
plea of friend or prayer of parent.

In her is all my relief,
I turn toward no other, no
other welcome in:
and ask nothing in turn
but that she keep faith.
That faith so fixed my courage
        and decided it,
that I have not the power to desire
any other love, whatever be it.

And when I say "my relief" don't
think it's only my pride, for
I so love and desire her that
if I had urgent business with Death,
        the robber,
I would not love God so well, nor
beg him to welcome me into Paradise,
        as I beg her she grant me
space of one whole night to lie beside her.

        But as I tell the truth, may He
        grant that I lie beside her.

RAIMON JORDAN

Translated from Provençal by Paul Blackburn

aucassin and nicolete imprisoned

NOW COUNT BOUGARS DE VALENCE made great war on Count Garin de Biaucaire. Never a day dawned on the lands of Biaucaire without the hundred knights and ten thousand horsemen and footmen of Count Bougars there at the gates, walls, and ramparts besieging the castle of Count Garin. His sole occupation and goal was to burn the count's land, spoil his country, and slay Garin's men.

Now the Count Garin de Biaucaire was old and frail, and his good days were over. He had no heir save his young son called Aucassin. His son was handsome and well-fashioned of body and limbs. His hair was yellow, in little curls; his eyes blue and laughing. His face fine and shapely, and so rich he appeared in all things good that there seemed to be no evil in him. But so much was he taken by Love, who is a great master of men and mover of things, that he would not, of his will, take arms or learn the ways of knighthood.

Therefore his mother and father said to him: "Son, go take thine arms, mount thy horse, and hold thy land. Help thy men, for if they see thee among them, more stoutly they will keep in battle their lives and lands, both thine and mine."

"Father," said Aucassin, "I marvel in the ways you speak. I will not be made knight, or face battle where knights smite and are smitten, unless thou give me Nicolete, the woman that I love so well."

"Son," said the father, "this may not be. Let Nicolete go. A slave girl is she, out of a strange land. The Captain of this town, who brought her from the Saracens and carried her hither, and hath reared her and hath christened the maid, and took her for his daughter in God, will one day find the right young man for her to win her bread honorably. Her though you ought not take for a wife, but if thou doest desire the daughter of a king or count, thou shalt have her."

"Father!" said Aucassin. "Tell me who among the courts of Germany, England, or France is more than her; so gentle is she and courteous and debonair and compact of all good qualities."

Then the Count Garin de Biaucaire knew that he could not withdraw Aucassin his son from the love of Nicolete. So he went to the Captain of the city, and spoke to him, saying: "Sir, I command thee to take away thy daughter in God, Nicolete; for by reason of her do I lose Aucassin, who will neither be dubbed knight nor do the things that fall to him to be done. And mark thee well," he said, "that if I might have her at my will, I would burn her in a fire and yourself might well be sore adread."

The Captain was grieved to hear such speech, but as it was the Count—his lord's—wishings, he promised to send her into a land and country where she might never be seen again.

So with this promise, they parted from each other. Now the Captain was a rich man. He had a rich palace with a garden in the midst of it, and into this palace he put Nicolete in an upper chamber with one old woman to keep her company. In the chamber he put bread and meat and wine and such things as were needful. Then he sealed the door, that none might come in or go forth, save that there was one window looking out on the garden, and straight enough, through which came to them a little air.

So through all the land the noise and speech was of how Nicolete was lost. Some said she had fled the country, and some that the Count Garin de Biaucaire had slain her.

So even though the Count Bougars had called up his knights and footmen and made for the castle to storm it, Aucassin was in his chamber sorrowing for Nicolete, his love. And though he heard the cry of battle arise, the din of knights and men-at-arms, and the shouts to hold the walls and gates, and the cries of anguish as the townsfolk mounted the battlements and cast down bolts and pikes, Aucassin continued making lament for Nicolete, his sweet lady whom he loved so well.

With the great assault at its height, Count Garin de Biaucaire entered the chamber of Aucassin and was angered to see his son lamenting so.

"Ha! son, how caitiff art thou, and cowardly, that can see men assail thy castle. Know thou that if thou lose it, thou losest all. Son, go to, take arms and mount thy horse. Defend thy land, help thy men, and fare thee well in battle. If they do but see thee among them, better will they guard their substance and their lives and thy land and mine. Art thou not so great and hardy of hands, that thou mightest do this one thing, as it is thy duty?"

So when he heard no answer, for he gathered in his son's looks a most stubborn desire to resign himself to Nicolete, he turned about. But as Aucassin saw him going he called to him, saying: "Father, I will make with thee fair covenant."

"What covenant, son?"

"I will take up arms and go into battle on this covenant, that, if God bring me back sound and safe, thou wilt let me see Nicolete, my sweet lady, even so long that I may have of her two words or three, and one kiss."

"That will I grant," said his father. At this was Aucassin glad.

Aucassin then armed himself and mounted his steed. How well he sat the shield on his shoulder, the helm on his head, and the baldric on his left haunch! Thus with his horse swift and keen, he spurred himself forth from the gate.

Now his mind was not on how he might strike a knight nor be stricken. Nay, no memory had Aucassin of knightly arms but of dreams of Nicolete, his sweet lady, so that he forgot all that a knight should do. Thus when he pressed into the foe, they laid hands on him all about and seized his spear and shield, and led him off a prisoner, and discoursed by what means of death he should die.

Thus when Aucassin heard them speak so, "Ha! God," said he, "sweet Savior. Be these my deadly enemies that have taken me and will soon cut off my head? Then no more shall I speak with Nicolete, my sweet lady, that I love so well. But as still have I a good sword and sit upon a horse unwearied, so let me keep my head for her love to love once again!"

Whereon he laid hand to sword and fell a-smiting to right and left, and smote through helm and nasal, and arm and clenched hand, making a murder about him, like a wild boar when hounds fall on him in the forest, even till he struck down ten knights, and seven he hurt, and straightway he hurled out of the enemy's hands, and rode back again at full speed, sword in hand.

Hearing they were about to hang Aucassin, his enemy, the Count Bougars de Valence came into view, and Aucassin was aware of him, and gat his sword into his hand, and lashed at his helm with such a stroke that the Count fell stunned and groveling. And then Aucassin laid hands on him, and brought him to his father.

"Father," quoth Aucassin, "lo! here is your mortal foe, who hath warred on you for full twenty years. Only for this man might this war be so ended."

"Good son," said his father, "feats of youth shouldst thou do, and not seek after folly."

"Father," saith Aucassin, "sermon me no sermons but fulfill my covenant."

"Ha! what covenant, son?"

"What, Father, hast thou forgotten it? Didst thou not make with me a covenant when I took up arms and went into battle, that if God brought me back safe and sound, thou wouldst let me see Nicolete, my sweet lady, even so long that I may have of her two words or three, and one kiss? So didst thou say, and my mind is that thou keep thy word."

"I!" quoth the father. "God forsake me if I keep this covenant! Nay, if she were here, I would let her burn in fire, and thyself shouldst be sore adread."

"Is this thy last word?" quoth Aucassin.

"So help me God," quoth his father, "yea!"

"This is a sorry thing meseems," quoth Aucassin, "when a man of thine age lies! Count de Valence! Give me thy hand."

"Sir, with good will."

So he set his hand in the other's.

"Now givest thou me thy word," said Aucassin, "that never whilst thou art a living man wilt thou avail to do my father dishonor, or harm him in body or in goods?"

"Yea, sir," quoth the Count Bougars.

"God help me ever, but I will make thy head fly from thy shoulders, if thou makest not troth," said Aucassin.

"In God's name," said he, "I will take thy oath."

So they did the oath, and Aucassin let him mount on a horse and then he returned himself to his father.

Here one singeth:

When the Count Garin doth know
That his child would ne'er forego
Love of her that loved him so,
Nicolete, the bright of brow,
In a dungeon deep below
Childe Aucassin did he throw.
Even there the Childe must dwell
In a dun-walled marble cell.
There he waileth in his woe
Crying thus as ye shall know:

"Nicolete, thou lily white,
Sweet thy footfall, sweet thine eyes,
And the mirth of thy replies,
Sweet thy laughter, sweet thy face,
Sweet thy lips, and sweet thy brow,

And the touch of thine embrace.
Who but doth in thee delight?
I for love of them am bound
In this dungeon underground,
All for loving thee must lie
Here were loud on thee I cry,
Here for loving thee must die
    For thee, my love,
      All for thee."

from AUCASSIN AND NICOLETE, Anonymous
Translated from French by Andrew Lang, adapted by the editor

from **"When, from the spring, the stream"**

My distant love, for you, my
    whole body aches:
and I can find nothing to heal it
    but in your call
    that has as bait
  soft love behind curtain or
  in orchard with the mate
    I long for.

That chance refused me forever, it's
    no wonder I burn.
There never was fairer lady, God
    couldn't want one,
Christian, Jewess, or Saracen.
The man who wins even a part of her love
    is fed on manna.

No end to my body's desire toward
　　　　her I love most.
I'm afraid my will will cheat me, over-
　　　　take me with lust;
for that pain is sharper than thorns and cured
　　　　only with joy.
I want pity from no one for a pain
　　　　I would share with no man. . . .

JAUFRÉ RUDEL

Translated from Provençal by Paul Blackburn

from **"When sere leaf falleth"**

Of love's wayfaring
　　　　I know no part to blame,
All other paring,
　　　　compared, is put to shame,
Man can acclaim
　　　　no second for comparing
With her, no dame
　　　　but hath the meaner bearing.

I'ld ne'er entangle
　　　　my heart with other fere,
Although I mangle
　　　　my joy by staying here
I have no fear
　　　　that ever at Pontrangle
You'll find her peer
　　　　or one that's worth a wrangle.

She'd ne'er destroy
  her man with cruelty
'Twixt here 'n' Savoy
  there feeds no fairer she,
Than pleaseth me
  till Paris had ne'er joy
In such degree
  from Helena in Troy.

She's so the rarest
  who holdeth me thus gay,
The thirty fairest
  can not contest her sway;
'Tis right, par fay,
  thou know. O song that wearest
Such bright array,
  whose quality thou sharest. . . .

ARNAUT DANIEL

Translated from Provençal by Ezra Pound

sir pelleas and the lady ettard

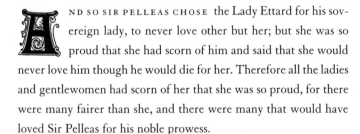

ND SO SIR PELLEAS CHOSE the Lady Ettard for his sovereign lady, to never love other but her; but she was so proud that she had scorn of him and said that she would never love him though he would die for her. Therefore all the ladies and gentlewomen had scorn of her that she was so proud, for there were many fairer than she, and there were many that would have loved Sir Pelleas for his noble prowess.

"And so this knight promised the Lady Ettard to follow her into this country of hers and never to leave her till she loved him. And thus he is here, and lodged by a priory, and every week she sendeth knights to fight with him. And when he hath put them to the ground, then will he suffer them wilfully to take him prisoner; because he would have a sight of this lady. And always she does him great despite, for sometimes she maketh her knights to tie him to his horse's tail, and sometimes to bind him under the horse's belly. Thus in the most shameful ways that she can think he is brought to her. And she does all this to cause him to leave this country, and to leave his loving; but all this cannot make him to leave."

So spoke Sir Carados.

"Alas," said Sir Gawain, "it is a great pity. After this night I will seek him tomorrow, in this forest, to do him all the help I can."

So on the morn Sir Gawain took his leave of his host, Sir Carados, and rode into the forest; and at the last he met with Sir Pelleas, who made great moan out of measure. Each of them saluted the other, and then Gawain asked him why he made such sorrow. And as it was told above, Sir Pelleas told Gawain.

"But always I suffer her knights to treat me so, in trust at the last to win her love, for she knoweth well all her knights should not win me; but I trust she will have pity upon me at the last, for love causeth many a good knight to suffer to have his will, but alas I am unfortunate."

And therewith Sir Pelleas made so great dole and sorrow that Gawain had to hold him on horseback.

"Now," said Sir Gawain, "leave your mourning and I shall promise you by the faith of my body to do all that lieth in my power to get you the love of your lady, and thereto I will plight you my troth."

"Ah," said Sir Pelleas, "of what court are ye? Tell me, I pray you, my good friend."

And then Sir Gawain said, "I am of the court of King Arthur, and his sister's son. And King Lot of Orkney was my father, and my name is Sir Gawain."

And then he said, "My name is Sir Pelleas, born in the Isles, and of many isles I am lord, and never have I loved lady nor damsel till now in an unhappy time; and, sir knight, since ye are cousin unto King Arthur, and a king's son, therefore betray me not but help me, for I may never come by her but by some good knight, for she is in a strong castle here, close within this four mile. Over all this country she is lady of."

"Well," said Sir Gawain, "all this shall I amend and ye will do as I shall devise: I will have your horse and your armor, and so will I ride unto her castle and tell her that I have slain you, and so shall I come within her to cause her to cherish me. Then shall I do my true part that ye shall not fail to have the love of her."

And therewith Sir Gawain plight his troth unto Sir Pelleas to be true and faithful unto him; so each one plight their troth to the other, and so they changed horses and harnesses, and Sir Gawain departed, and came to the castle where stood the pavilions of this lady outside the gate. And as soon as Ettard had espied Sir Gawain she fled in toward the castle.

Sir Gawain spake on high and bade her abide, for he was not Sir Pelleas: "I am another knight that have slain Sir Pelleas."

"Do off your helm," said the Lady Ettard, "that I may see your visage."

And so when she saw that it was not Sir Pelleas, she bade him alight and, leading him unto her castle, asked him faithfully whether he had slain Sir Pelleas. And he told her yea, and told her his name was Sir Gawain of the court of King Arthur and the son of Arthur's sister as well.

"Truly," said she, "that is great pity, for he was a passing good knight of his body, but of all men alive I hated him most, for I could never be quit of him; and for ye have slain him I shall be your woman, and to do anything that might please you." So she made Sir Gawain good cheer.

Then Sir Gawain said that he loved a lady and by no means would she love him.

"She is to blame," said Ettard, "for ye that be so well born a man, and such a man of prowess, there is no lady in the world too good for you."

"Will ye," said Sir Gawain, "promise me to do all that ye may, by the faith of your body, to get me the love of my lady?"

"Yea, sir," said she, "and that I promise you by the faith of my body."

"Now," said Sir Gawain, "it is yourself that I love so well, therefore I pray you hold your promise."

"I may not choose," said the Lady Ettard, "but if I should be false." And so she granted him to fulfill all his desire.

So it was then in the month of May that she and Sir Gawain went out of the castle and supped in a pavilion, and there was made a bed; and there Sir Gawain and the Lady Ettard went to bed together. In another pavilion she laid her damsels, and in the third pavilion she laid part of her knights, for then she had no dread of Sir Pelleas. And there Sir Gawain lay with her in that pavilion two days and two nights. And on the third day, in the morning early, Sir Pelleas armed himself, for he had never slept since Sir Gawain departed from him; for Sir Gawain had promised him by the faith of his body to come to him unto his pavilion by that priory within the space of a day and a night.

Then Sir Pelleas mounted upon horseback and came to the pavilions that stood without the castle. He found in the first pavilion three knights in three beds and three squires lying at their feet. Then went he to the second pavilion and found four gentlewomen lying in four beds. And then he came to the third pavilion and found Sir Gawain lying in bed with his Lady Ettard, with each in the other's arms, and when he saw that his heart well-nigh burst for sorrow.

"Alas!" he cried, "that ever a knight should be found so false"; and then he took his horse for he could abide no longer for pure sorrow. And when he had ridden nigh half a mile he turned again and thought to slay them both; but when he saw them both so lie sleeping fast, he said to himself, "Though this knight be never so false, I will never slay him sleeping, for I will never destroy the high order of knighthood."

And therewith he departed again. But he had only ridden half a mile when he returned again and thought once more to slay them both. Making the greatest sorrow that ever man made, he came to the pavilions and, tying his horse unto a tree, pulled out his sword naked in his hand. He went to them there as they lay, and yet he thought it were a shame to slay them sleeping. And so he laid the naked sword overthwart both their throats and took his horse and so rode his way.

When Sir Gawain and Ettard awoke of their sleep and found the naked sword overthwart their throats, Ettard knew well it was Sir Pelleas's sword.

"Alas!" said she to Sir Gawain, "ye have betrayed me and Sir Pelleas both, for ye told me ye had slain him, and now I know well it is not so—he is alive. And if Sir Pelleas had been as uncourteous to you as ye have been to him ye had been a dead knight; but ye have deceived me and betrayed me falsely, that all ladies and damsels may beware by you and me." And therewith Sir Gawain made himself ready and went into the forest.

So it happed then that the Damsel of the Lake, Nimue, met with a knight of Sir Pelleas, who went on foot in the forest making great dole, and she asked him the cause. And so the woeful knight told her how his master and lord was betrayed through a knight and lady, and how he will never arise out of his bed till he be dead.

"Bring me to him," said she, "and I will warrant his life he shall not die for love, and she that hath caused him so to love, she shall be in as evil plight as he, for it is no joy of such a proud lady that will have no mercy on such a valiant knight."

So that knight brought her unto him, and when she saw him lie in his bed, she thought she saw never so likely a knight; and therewith she threw an enchantment upon him, and he fell asleep and charged no man to awake him till she came again. And therewhile she rode unto the Lady Ettard. So within two hours she brought the Lady Ettard thither, and both ladies found him asleep.

"Lo," said the Damsel of the Lake, "ye ought to be ashamed for to murder such a knight."

And therewith she threw such an enchantment upon her that she loved him sore, that well-nigh she was out of her mind.

"O Lord Jesus," said the Lady Ettard, "how is it befallen unto me that I love now him that I have most hated of any man alive?"

"That is the righteous judgment of God," said the damsel.

And then anon Sir Pelleas awaked and looked upon Ettard; and when he saw her he knew her, and then he hated her more than any woman alive, and said: "Away, traitress, come never in my sight." And when she heard him say so, she wept and made great sorrow out of measure.

"Sir knight Pelleas," said the Damsel of the Lake, "take your horse and come forth with me out of this country, and ye shall love a lady that shall love you."

"I will well," said Sir Pelleas, "for this Lady Ettard hath done me great despite and shame." And there he told her the beginning and ending, and how he had purposed never to have arisen till that he had been dead. "And now such grace God hath sent me, that I hate her as much as ever I loved her, thanks be our Lord Jesus!"

"Thank me," said the Damsel of the Lake.

Anon Sir Pelleas armed himself and took his horse and commanded his men to bring his pavilions and his provisions where the Damsel of the Lake would reside. So the Lady Ettard died for sorrow, and the Damsel of the Lake rejoiced in Sir Pelleas, and they loved together during their life days.

from LE MORTE D'ARTHUR by Sir Thomas Malory

Adapted by the editor

"I think sometimes about"

I think sometimes about
what I would tell her
if I were near enough.
It makes the miles shorter
to call my sorrow out
to her, with thoughts.
Often the people here
see in me the figure
of a carefree man,
for so I let it seem.

Had I not taken on
such lofty love,
I might be saved.
I did it without thinking.
And every moment now I suffer
pain that presses deep.
Now my own constancy
has tied down my heart
and will not let it part
from her, as things are now.

It is a great wonder:
she whom I love with greatest torment
has always acted like my enemy.
Now may no man ever get to know
what such a burden is,
it weighs down hard.

I thought I knew what it was before,
now I know it better.
Over there, where home is, I was sad,
and here three times more.

However little good it does me,
still I have this pleasure:
no one can stop me
from thinking close to her,
wherever on earth I turn.
This comfort she must let me have.
If she takes it well,
that gives me joy forever,
for I, more than any other man,
was always hers.

FRIEDRICH VON HAUSEN

Translated from German by Frederick Goldin

Lost Love

IN THE TALE of SIR ORFEO, the hero struggles and succeeds in re-capturing in life a love that death has set claim to. But many of the poets here, seeing the futility of struggling against death, mark the passing of a loved one in song—a lasting testament to the glory of a love that was.

∾ "Song seizes me, but my own vers gives me dolor"
    Guillem IX (1071-1127)

∾ A Lady laments for her lost Lover, by similitude of a Falcon
    Anonymous (dates unknown)

∾ "How closely to you would I cling"
    Lady of Castelozza (born c. 1200)

∾ SIR LANCEOR AND HIS LADY COLOMBE
    From *Le Morte D'Arthur* by Sir Thomas Malory (d. 1471)

∾ Of the Grave of Selvaggia, on the Monte della Sambuca
    Cino da Pistoia (1270-1337)

∾ *from* Of his Dead Lady
    Giacomino Pugliesi, Knight of Prato (mid-13th century)

∾ SIR ORFEO
    Anonymous (dates unknown)

∾ "If you would know the reason why"
    Bertrand d'Alamonon (late 13th century)

"Song seizes me, but my own vers gives me dolor"

Song seizes me, but my own vers gives me dolor,
and in Poitou or Limousin I'll never again be lover.

To exile now, fearful in mid of danger,
and leave my son to fight those who will give him hurt.

I lose both heart and possession quitting Poitou;
I leave Folque d'Anjou to guard the land and his cousin.

If Folque cannot hold it, he who grants me seisin*   *protection
will have Angevins and Gascons on his neck.

They will see him young and feeble when I have gone
they will bring him down if his prowess be not double.

Mercy I ask of friends wherever I have wronged:
I pray to Christ in Occitan, also in Latin.

I rode in prowess and joy, leave both behind now
going hellbent to where all sinners end up.

Gaily I lived. Now God no longer cares for it:
being half-dead, even I no longer desire it.

All ceremony quit, all loving habit:
if God love me, whatever comes, I welcome it.

Friends, at my demise come do me honor:
since I've taken my pleasure all over the neighborhood too.

All gracious show I leave, joys of love and table,
two kinds of grey fur, also sable.

GUILLEM IX

Translated from Provençal by Paul Blackburn

A Lady laments for her lost Lover, by similitude of a Falcon

Alas for me, who loved a falcon well!
  So well I loved him, I was nearly dead:
  Ever at my low call he bent his head,
And ate of mine, not much, but all that fell.
Now he has fled, how high I cannot tell,
  Much higher now than ever he has fled,
  And is in a fair garden housed and fed;
Another lady, alas! shall love him well.
Oh, my own falcon whom I taught and rear'd!
  Sweet bells of shining gold I gave to thee
That in the chase thou shouldst not be afeard.
  Now thou hast risen like the risen sea,
Broken thy jesses* loose, and disappear'd,   *straps
  As soon as thou wast skilled in falconry.

ANONYMOUS

Translated from Italian by Dante Gabriel Rossetti

"How closely to you would I cling"

How closely to you would I cling;
  How quickly your falsehood forget;
And praises alone of you sing,
  Could you be sincere even yet!

To coquetry did I resort
  They say 'twould your constancy win;
But that were just censure to court,
  And give you excuse for your sin.

From a heart that refuses to melt
Those who bid me my feelings conceal,
A passion like mine never felt;
A passion like mine cannot feel.

To censure my passionate sighs,
I'm sure that there would be but few,
If you they could see with mine eyes,
Or dwell on your lips as I do.

Never out of my thoughts is that night
When you said you'd be mine ne'er to part.
On that promise I dwell with delight;
'Tis the dream—the fond dream of my heart!

No envoy I send, but declare
In person, I hope not in vain,
No shelter have I from despair
If you will persist in disdain.

As you wish to be honored below;
As you hope to find favor above;
On your suppliant mercy bestow,
Nor let her die martyred of Love!

LADY OF CASTELOZZA

Translated from Provençal by John Rutherford

sir lanceor and his lady colombe

HERE WAS A KNIGHT WHO was the Irish king's son and his name was Lanceor, a proud knight, who counted himself one of the best of the court; and he had great despite of Balin for winning that sword from the damsel's scabbard which no other man could claim, thus accounting him more hardy, more of prowess. And he had despite against Balin for the shame he brought on King Arthur's court by slaying in their presence the Lady of the Lake. Thus he asked King Arthur if he would give him leave to ride after Balin and to revenge the despite that he had done. "Do your best," said Arthur, "I am right wroth with Balin; I would he were quit of the wrong that he hath done to me and to my court." Then this Lanceor went to his lodgings to make himself ready.

So the knight of Ireland armed him at all points, and dressed his shield on his shoulder, and mounted upon horseback, and took his spear in his hands and rode after him at a great pace, as much as his horse might go; and within a mile or so he had close sight of Balin, and with a loud voice he cried, "Abide, knight, for ye shall abide whether ye will or not, and the shield that is before you shall not help."

When Balin heard this, he turned his horse fiercely, and said, "Fair knight, what will ye with me, will ye joust with me?"

"Yes," said the Irish knight, "that is why I come after you."

"Maybe," said Balin, "it had been better to have kept you at home, for many a man tries to put his enemy to a rebuke, but often it falleth back unto himself."

"Of what court be ye sent from?" said Balin.

"I am come from the court of King Arthur," said the knight of Ireland, "and come hither for to revenge the despite ye did this day to King Arthur, and to his court."

"Well," said Balin, "I see well I must have ado with you, but your quarrel is full simple unto me, for the Lady of the Lake, who is dead, did me great wrong by slaying my mother, else would I have been loath as any knight to slay a lady."

"Make you ready," said the knight Lanceor, "and dress you unto me, for only one shall abide in the field."

Then they took their spears, and came together as much as their horses might drive. The Irish knight smote Balin on the shield, that all went shivers off his spear, and Balin hit him through the shield, and the hauberk perished, and so pierced through his body and the horse's croup. Anon he turned his horse fiercely, and drew out his sword, as he knew not that he had slain him; and then he saw him lie as a dead corpse.

And as he looked, then was he ware of a damsel that came riding full fast as her horse might ride. And when she espied that Lanceor was slain, she made sorrow out of measure, and said, "O Balin, two bodies thou hast slain and one heart, and two hearts in one body, and two souls thou hast lost."

And therewith she took the sword from her love that lay dead, and fell to the ground in a swoon. And when she arose she made great dole out of measure, which sorrow grieved Balin passingly sore, and he went unto her for to take the sword out of her hand, but she held it so fast he might not take it out of her hand unless he should have hurt her, and then suddenly she set the pommel to the ground, and drove the sword through her body.

When Balin espied her deeds, he was passing heavy in his heart, and ashamed that so fair a damsel had destroyed herself for love. "Alas," said Balin, "me repenteth sore the death of this knight and for the love of his damsel, for there was much true love betwixt them both." And to no longer behold this sorrow, he turned his horse and looked toward a great forest.

Then there came a dwarf from the city of Camelot on horseback, as much as he might, and found the dead bodies, wherefore he made great dole, and pulled out his hair for sorrow, and said, "Hast you knight done this deed?"

"Why askest thou?" said Balin. "It was I that slew this knight in my defense, for hither he came to chase me, and either I must slay him or he me; and this damsel slew herself for his love, which repenteth me, and for her sake I shall owe all women the better love."

"Alas," said the dwarf, "thou hast done great damage unto thyself, for this knight that is here dead was one of the most valorous men that lived."

So as they talked, there came the king of Cornwall, King Mark, riding. And when he saw these two bodies dead, and heard the knight's and the dwarf's tale about how they died, then made the king great sorrow for the true love that was betwixt them, and said, "I will not depart till I have on his earth made a tomb." And there he put his pavilions and sought through all the country to find a tomb, and in a church they found one that was fair and rich, and then the king put them both in the earth, and put the tomb upon them, and wrote the names of them both on the tomb.

The meanwhile as this was a-doing in came Merlin to King Mark and, seeing all his doing, said, "Here shall be in this same place the greatest battle betwixt two knights that was or ever shall be, and the truest lovers, and yet none of them shall slay other." And there Merlin wrote their names upon the tomb with letters of gold that should fight in that place, whose names were Lancelot de Lake and Tristan.

And King Mark marveled that any man save Merlin should speak of such wondrous deeds.

from LE MORTE D'ARTHUR by Sir Thomas Malory

Adapted by the editor

Of the Grave of Selvaggia, on the Monte della Sambuca

I was upon the high and blessed mound,
    And kissed, long worshipping, the stones and grass,
    There on the hard stones prostrate, where, alas!
That pure one laid her forehead in the ground.
Then were the springs of gladness sealed and bound,
    The day that unto Death's most bitter pass
    My sick heart's lady turned her feet, who was
Already in her gracious life renown'd.
So in that place I spake to Love, and cried:
    'O sweet my god, I am one whom Death may claim
      Hence to be his; for lo! my heart lies here.'
      Anon, because my Master lent no ear,
    Departing, still I called Selvaggia's name.
So with my moan I left the mountain-side.

CINO DA PISTOIA

Translated from Italian by Dante Gabriel Rossetti

from **Of his Dead Lady**

Death, why hast thou made life so hard to bear,
    Taking my lady hence? Hast thou no whit
Of shame? The youngest flower and the most fair
    Thou hast plucked away, and the world wanteth it.
O leaden Death, hast thou no pitying?
Our warm love's very spring
    Thou stopp'st, and endest what was holy and meet;

And of my gladdening
Mak'st a most woful thing,
And in my heart dost bid the bird not sing
     That sang so sweet. . . .

O God, why hast thou made my grief so deep?
     Why set me in the dark to grope and pine?
Why parted me from her companionship,
     And crushed the hope which was a gift of thine?
To think, dear, that I never any more
Can see thee as before!
     Who is it shuts thee in?
Who hides that smile for which my heart is sore,
And drowns those words that I am longing for,
     Lady of mine?

Where is my lady, and the lovely face
     She had, and the sweet motion when she walk'd?—
Her chaste, mild favour—her so delicate grace—
     Her eyes, her mouth, and the dear way she talk'd?—
Her courteous bending—her most noble air—
The soft fall of her hair? . . .
My lady—she to whom my soul
     A gladness brought!
Now I do never see her anywhere,
And may not, looking in her eyes, gain there
     The blessing which I sought. . . .

GIACOMINO PUGLIESI, KNIGHT OF PRATO

Translated from Italian by Dante Gabriel Rossetti

SIR ORFEO

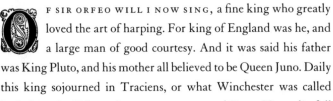F SIR ORFEO WILL I NOW SING, a fine king who greatly loved the art of harping. For king of England was he, and a large man of good courtesy. And it was said his father was King Pluto, and his mother all believed to be Queen Juno. Daily this king sojourned in Traciens, or what Winchester was called back then. And his precious queen was named Dame Heurodis; full of such love and goodness no one questioned her fairness.

Well in the beginning of May, when merry and hot is the day, and gone are the harsh winter showers, and every field is full of flowers, this queen, Dame Heurodis, and two lovely maidens set out for the orchard of blossoming flowers to hear the lovely birds sing. So they set themselves down all three beneath the boughs of a fair grafted-tree, when the fair queen did start sleeping. So she slept and slept till it was noon when the maidens thought it best to wake her soon. Yet before they could make her awake, the queen opened her eyes and cried and cried and made horrible sounds that came out strange and wild. She tore at her gentle hands and feet, and scratched at her visage and made it bleed. Her rich stained robe was totally ripped and then she screamed and lost her wits. The two maidens beside her, all full of fright, then ran off to find a squire or knight.

So soon all to the orchard they ran, knights and ladies and lovely maidens. They seized her wild arms and at last brought her to bed where ropes held her fast.

So there she stayed, though she wept swift and quick as she lay. And then said the queen, "Alas, my lord Orfeo! how have I loved thee! and you . . . me! My love, since we were first together never was there a fight between us ever. Yet now I must face my fiercest foe, so no longer will we be one, but on my own must I go!"

"Alas," quoth he, "if this mad talk be so—who is this foe? Yet do not fear for wherever thou art I will go with thee, and wherever

I go thou shall go with me. Forever and ever we'll together be, so will our love always lasting see."

"Nay . . . Nay, that I can't see," said Queen Heurodis. "I will tell thee truly how it is! As I lay this morning beneath an orchard tree, two fair knights, well-armed and strong, came to me. They bid me to go with them and their king, but I answered them bold and loudly, 'I dare not, nor never will I go with you or your king!' Then came their king with a hundred knights or more and a hundred damsels as well and all on milk-white steeds they traveled. Never such a thing before had I seen. Soon as their king came upon me, he grabbed my arms and feet and then seized me. So with him I rode upon his steed and at his side to his palace where I was to reside. He showed me his castles, his gardens with flowers, his flowing waters, and his rich lands. Then he brought me home again to our own orchard, and said to me afterward:

" 'Tomorrow thou will be right here under this orchard tree, and with us thou shalt go, for no thing will hinder thee.' "

"Nay!" King Orfeo screamed. "Never shall I leave thee, my wife. Never shall I lose to another my queen, my life!"

So tomorrow came with its morning, and Orfeo's thousand knights sat by the orchard trees, each stout and grim, each armed and waiting. A shelter of soldiers stood on each side, and by their precious queen would they abide. And all day they stood under the sun, but of the queen, the men never saw what she had become. For truly, she was gone, and just as the day had dawned.

So there was a great crying, weeping, and woe, as the king into his chamber made go and often he wept upon the stones and cried out his soul and made such a moan. For this day's strange enchantment, he wept all night till his life was near spent.

Then he got together his barons and earls the next morn and he made known thus saying, "From us the greatest queen is forlorn. Aie! the fairest lady that ever was born. A king, I can no longer be. So I order my Steward to rule from here afterward. Away will I go into the wilderness where I will find my Dame Heurodis. If you ever hear my life's been spent, then make you new parliament and choose among you a king. Thus I leave you with all of my things."

Though there was great weeping in the hall, he bid good-bye to them all. And he put on a pilgrim's mantle and hood, and though he had this warm wool coat, upon himself he had no other good. So that he who once had castles and towers, rivers, forests, and gardens with flowers, now found no thing for his ease, but now must sleep on the cold ground and freeze. And he who had many a wise man for his ills, must now dig for roots for his fill.

Lord! who may tell the sores this king held for ten years or more. His harp where he had all his glee he hid for safe keeping in the hollow trunk of a tree; and when the weather was clear and bright, his harping did seem to make things alright. For all the wild beasts that he saw around seemed to make joy and pleasant sounds. And when he of his harping let go, none of these wild beasts would show.

Then he saw the fairy king making route and hunting with all his knights about. And he'd also seen among those of the king his own Dame Heurodis! A strange thing that would be for him that is. He beheld her and he did her eyes seek, but no word could she say or speak. For a maiden brought her away to ride, for with him no longer could she reside.

"Alas," quoth he, "great is my woe. For God's sake, why is my death so slow! Aie! too long is my life, when I dare not talk with my wife, nor she to me one word speak. O that my eyes might no longer see!"

Then with his harp he set off to find his wife, those knights and ladies, and that fairy king. Then into a rock he saw the ladies ride and there he went also to find where they abide. Then he came into fair country, smooth and plain and all green—neither hill nor dale did he ever see. And before him a castle he sights, rich and royal and of wonderful heights, and all of the outermost walls were made clear like glass crystal. And therein he saw his wife, Dame Heurodis, the love of his life.

So after he beheld these marvels all, he went into the king's great hall. Then he saw there a curious sight—a tabernacle blissful and bright. And therein was the king set, and his queen, fair and quiet. And when he beheld in this hall everything, then he kneeled down before the great king.

"O lord," he said, "if thy will it I will make thee wonderful music."

And the king answered, "Who art thou that ye come to my kingdom now?"

"Lord," quoth he, "please know full well, I am just but a poor minstrel. And sire, it is the manner of us all to seek many a great lord's house; though we not always welcome be, yet still we must offer up our glee."

And before the king could sit down, he made of his harp so merry a sound and sung with harp as well as he could so soon all in the palace around him stood. The king heard and stood full still as for these sounds he had good will. So when he stopped with his harping then to him said the king, "Minstrel, me liketh well thy glee, so ask of me what will it be? Largely will I pay thee, so come speak and try me."

"Sir," he said, "I beseech thee, that thou would give me that bright lady with bright eyes, that woman, the Dame Heurodis."

"Nay" quoth the king, "thou art lean and loathsome and she is of fair complexion. A lowly thing it would be for her to be seen with you in rags together!"

"O Sire," he said, "gentle king, yet it were a fouler thing to hear a lie from you sound than me here in rags just now. All I ask if I could is that you keep now to your word."

So saith the king, "Since it is so, take her by the hand and go."

Then his wife he took by her hand, and made swift journey out of that land. So long in the forest had he made his way that he knew the roads to Winchester, though long had he been away.

He came to his city but no one knew it was he. All saw his harp and wondered if the life of their king had been sundered. Then all let out a large cry for it was indeed the harp they espied. And then they thought their lord quite dead, but of all his Steward showed the greatest dread. So Sir Orfeo knew well by this deed his Steward was his successor to be. And he loved him now and stood him up, saying, "Thou, Steward, listen to this thing! I am Sir Orfeo, your king! Yet for all of your love I think, if I had never returned you'd be a great king."

So then with grand procession, they brought them through the town with all manner of minstrelsy. Lord! there was such a melody! For joy all wept with their eyes, and then with their hearts joined it with sighs.

Now King Orfeo newly crowned is, and with his queen, Dame Heurodis, they lived long happily afterward, and then made their king the Steward.

After that the harpers in Britain, hearing how this grand tale began, made a lay of their liking and named it after this great king. The lay "Orfeo" they wrote; good is the lay, sweet the note. Thus came "Sir Orfeo" out of their care that may God grant to all good fare!

ANONYMOUS

Adapted from Middle English by the editor

"If you would know the reason why"

If you would know the reason why
But half a song I bring,
I have—alas, I must reply—
But half a theme to sing!
'Tis I alone that feel the spell;
'Tis I alone that burn:
The lady that I love so well
My love will not return.

I'll take the "No" she deigns to give,
Since she withholds the "Yes;"
Better with her in hope to live
Than elsewhere to possess!
Since with my fate I cannot cope,
Shall this my solace prove—
To dream that she, as whispers hope,
May one day learn to love.

BERTRAND D'ALAMONON

Translated from Provençal by John Rutherford

The Perilous Mirror

WHETHER THE POET sees a reflection of himself in his beloved's eyes, or a garden of wonder in a crystal fountain, these enchanting images remain perilous. For entwined with these reflections is an emptiness that can lead the poet into despair. Yet, as shown in the story from The Romance of the Rose, *finding a means past these perils can disclose to the poet the realms of tenderness and rage that Love commands.*

❁ IN THE GARDEN OF SIR MIRTH
  from the first book of *The Romance of the Rose* by Guillaume de Lorris (mid-13th century)

❁ "When I see the lark move"
  Bernart de Ventadorn (1148-1195)

❁ "It has gone with me as with a child"
  Heinrich von Morungen (d. 1222)

❁ *from* He finds that Love has beguiled him, but will trust in his Lady
  Simbuono Giudice (mid-13th century)

❁ "My lady carries love within her eyes"
  Dante Alighieri (1265-1321)

in the Garden of Sir Mirth

The dreamer of this poem, who is also its author, found in this ecstatic dream such a resemblance to love's experience among the waking hours that the poet deemed it fitting to recall under Love's authority this adventure in sleep. And so for her, his lover, a noble flower, he made this affair and named it The Romance of the Rose.

THIS DREAM I DREAMED occurred in May, a month wherein Love excites all living things in his delight. The earth, no longer enduring winter's cold expanse, exalts in her new threads of the finest colors prized. The bird's song instructs all but the hardest of hearts to love, as the young eagerly follow their plaintive call.

It was in this season, asleep one evening, that this dream I dreamed stirred. And to a light within this dream, I arose. The daylight never seemed so bright. With a silver needle threaded with silk in hand, I basted my sleeves as I walked out of town. Bird songs filled the solemn morning air. And I was so happy though I was alone.

A bright, clear river then appeared. Against the sun it looked to be silver. The stones beneath its water flow so dazzled me I thought to see in them faces smiling. I loved this river. Gladly, I followed wherever it led me. Astride its banks, I walked with its rippling waves. And at its side, a garden I saw. A garden with high embattled walls, painted with portraits of sordid sorts framed in gold and blue. Hideous, yet carefully portrayed. So many were there, I will tell you of this wall. Now let me see, which ones do I recall . . .

Hate and Felony . . . Villainy . . . yes, those were three
    their faces frowning   with frenzied eyes
       and brows proud
   . . . and then there was   Covetousness
   with pursed lips   bent over   and knotted hands

 and Avarice   covered in rags   weak and lean
   a cloak badly torn   a complexion leak-green
     her shrunken limbs   worn out and poor

    Envy   sad and unsmiling
  a disdaining   sideways glance of the eyes

 Sorrow   emaciated   pale   and jaundiced
her cheeks streaked with red lines her fingernails wrought
her eyes filled with dolor   a torn robe and her hair distraught

and then followed   Poverty   Hypocrisy   and   Old Age

Never did a man arrive to these walls in a crude state of mind. So precise and high and finely made, they did intimidate. And beyond them in the garden—more bird songs and savory flowers than I've ever heard or seen before. To enter this garden was my only goal. Yet there were no openings or doors—only a small wicket gate barred.

Then after many knocks, a maiden answered and she opened this gate. She was so striking, so well arrayed, she seemed to be in person the lusty month of May. She had no other care but to groom and fashion her hair. Her name, Dame Idleness, she called herself. And she went on to explain that Sir Mirth was lord of this garden. He made these walls and had those sorrowful images painted so that he might with his friends find diversion. Then after I asked kindly of her to let me enter, she let me in. It was an earthly paradise, spiritual with birds for its angels. Greatly I desired to see Sir Mirth. So down a path, fringed with mint and fennel, she led me.

When I saw him and his company, I knew this was no ordinary party. They began a carol led by a woman named Gladness. Her voice was as sweet and cool as vanilla ice. Hearing it, my blood warmed. Next was a song of Lorraine accompanied by jugglers and girls with tambourines. They were such a happy folk, I could have lived my life filled with their heavenly whims. So then a fair damsel named Courtesy bid me to join in on their joyous affair. As asked, I began to dance and, with the others, joined hands.

During this dance, I began to notice the shape and manners of all the folk that were there, and I shall tell you who they were. First was Sir Mirth, long and of good height, a fair mouth, and his eyes quite bright. He seemed so agile, so jolly of mien, you could imagine him a noble portraiture. For fun, his lover placed a wreath of roses about his hair. And Dame Gladness was his slender mistress. She sung so well with glad courage, that since they were twelve years of age, to him her love she granted. She held Sir Mirth's finger and he hers as they danced. Great was the love between them, like two new roses they seemed. Then next to her the God of Love stood. He, who can bring down the conceited and the proud, wore a robe of flowers—periwinkle, broom, violet, and others were all interlaced with rose leaves, long and broad. And above his head he wore a chaplet with nightingales, finches, larks, and other like—birds flying always nearby. The most angelic of them all, he seemed as if he came down direct from heaven. Besides him was his friend, Mr. Sweet Looks, a bachelor who held Love's arrows, five of which were of good wood and golden arrowheads, and five of which were of crooked, knotted wood with arrowheads of iron. The golden arrows inspired good, while the later arrows brought cruelty. Then behind him followed Beauty, whom the God of Love favored most, then Wealth with her paramour, a handsome, well-dressed horse-trainer, and then came Lady Largesse, and her lover, a knight, a kin of King Arthur. Still this dance continued with the Lady Franchise, who had for a lover a young man who did not give his name, but seemed to be some lord of Windsor. Now followed Courtesy and her man, a fair knight, and then came Idleness, who was my partner. The last of them that I remember was Youth, who spent his time innocently kissing his love, so sweetly, they were like two turtledoves. Of these fair and genteel dancers, I have just named but some.

Yet, I was curious of this garden. I longed to see the rest. So I made my absence from lovely Idleness and the dance. Great was my desire to know of its herbs, fruits, flowers, and trees—Was this why the God of Love pursued me? As I left the dance, I saw him with Mr. Sweet Looks spying on me. As I wandered among the trees listening to the birds and watching the rabbits feed, his gaze was directed straight at me. I continued aimlessly, but if I was his target what was he waiting for? Not once did he ask from Mr. Sweet Looks his bows and arrows, his instruments of power.

Then at last I reached the fairest spot in all of the garden. It was a flowing spring beneath a towering pine tree. A natural fountain with a clever marble well wherein was written on its border, "Here was where Fair Narcissus fell."

A victim of himself, I knew the story well. Careful was I not to gaze into that spring. I withdrew, but then again, what did I have to fear? I was smart and scholarly—hardly a Narcissus. So telling myself thus, I kneeled down to see this Perilous Mirror.

O what a fountain! The water clear, always lightly flowing, mounting two fingers in height, feeding the tender grass nearby, keeping it green. And in its basin were cleverly set, two crystal stones reflecting blue, yellow, red, and other rich hues. Quite a marvel! Yet these crystals also had the power to see all the garden's trees, flowers, and lovely greens. From any glance, this fountain mirrored one of the garden's endless details.

This was indeed the Perilous Mirror of Narcissus. Everything reflected there one could not help but to dearly love. The splendors of the garden I viewed but . . . Ah misery! There . . . I saw myself!

Quickly, I averted my eyes back to the thousands of images reflected there. Not wanting to follow that tragic young man, I focused instead on a rose bush full with a thousand flowers, enclosed by a thorny hedge. So great was my lust after so long a gaze on the reflection of this rose bush that I sent myself into a rage. So I then turned toward this rose bush, and once I was close by, its aroma overwhelmed me. Just one budding rose, not two days open, was all I desired, but its surrounding hedge of nettles and thorns kept me at bay.

'Cause of that one budding rose out of a thousand rose flowers, I stood there troubled by the thorns. How did I know this was the moment the God of Love had been waiting for? He strung his bow and, from Mr. Sweet Looks, took an arrow, aimed, and shot straight into my eye. This arrow then traveled right to my heart. It was the golden arrow named Beauty that pierced me. I shivered and thought of my blood to have lost plenty, but no gore around me did I see. So then again I lusted after that one budding rose, but before I could turn, the God of Love shot another arrow through my eye, piercing my heart. This time, it was named Simplicity, another golden arrowhead. All around I saw no doctor, but lo! what did it matter, for this wound there was no cure. One budding rose is all I thought of, when O! Another arrow! Now named Courtesy. And then straight in succession did I feel two more blows. Company and Fair-Seeming were the arrows. Strange was their power, the way they mingled weal with woe. I despaired greatly that they ever could be removed.

The God of Love seeing me in such thralls, then walked over and with a special ointment relieved me somewhat. Its sole cure was the sorrow it allowed me to endure. After seeing that I would not die, the God of Love then told me, "You are now by my arrows held, so don't rebel or do something foolish or else you'll only hurt yourself. Your pride now is worthless. So listen to what I desire." To this I could only answer, "Sir, at your bidding I would yield myself in all things. Into your service I take myself; God forbid I should make any resistence. For to fulfill your liking, and to have only from you your Mercy, is all that I desire."

Then he took me by my hand and raised me up, saying, "What you have said did please me much. No villain or scoundrel could come up with such pleasant words. You seem to be a man of substance. Thus I grant to you to do what no base man will ever do— press your lips to mine, and then the greatest honor will be with you. For with me as your Master, you shall always have a kind and gentle heart nearby."

With that, I rose and clasped my hands, and kissed him on the mouth. It had such mirth and liking that there and then I lost much of what I had languished in. Then for this touch, he demanded from me something dear. "Sire," I replied, "I do not know why you ask from me what is already in your keeping. My heart is yours, in both thought and deed. For from you I do feel such justice that my heart being yours is only so much wiser. Yet, if you still doubt my loyalty, make my heart your prisoner and you the keeper of the key."

"With this I'm fully in accord," quoth Love. "For full lord of the body is he who has heart for his treasure. Of this, I could ask no more." So saying, he removed from his splendid robe a golden key and then he touched my side so softly I could barely feel the key that speared my heart and locked it solid.

So it was in this way that the dreamer and author of this poem also found himself its lover.

from the first book of THE ROMANCE OF THE ROSE by
Guillame de Lorris
Translated from French by Geoffrey Chaucer, adapted by the editor

"When I see the lark move"

When I see the lark move
In joy his wings against the light
And then forget himself and fall in the air,
Sweetness having entered his heart,
I start envying
All that rejoices,
And marvel that my heart
Doesn't melt from desiring.

I thought I knew so much about love,
And I know so little:
I can't stop loving
Her from whom I'll never have love.
She took my heart, she took myself from me,
And took herself, and she took the whole world,
And when she took herself she left behind nothing
But desire, and a heart that keeps wanting.

I've lost all self-control,
I'm not myself
Ever since you let me look into your eyes:
Into a mirror that pleases me.
Mirror, since I saw myself in you
Sighs from inside have risen and slain me.
I got lost, the way Narcissus
Lost track of himself in that pool.

I give up on women,
I'll never trust a woman again.
As much as I've loved them,
That much I'll hold back love.

Not one offered to help me
Against her who ruins and destroys me.
I don't trust one of them,
They're all the same.

My lady shows she's a woman
And I hold it against her:
She doesn't want what she should want
And what she's not supposed to do, she does.
I've made a mess,
I've acted like the fool on the bridge.
And I don't know why this happens to me:
Unless it's because I always go too far.

Mercy is gone,
And I've never even known mercy.
She who I thought had most
Has least: where else look for it?
Everyone who sees her condemns her:
This poor lovestruck fool
Can't find any luck without her
And she lets him die, and doesn't help him.

My lady doesn't care about anything,
Not prayers, or pleading, or the rights I've earned.
Since she gets no pleasure from my love
I won't keep repeating myself.
I'll say goodbye and give up everything:
She caused my death and by death I'll reply.
And I'll go away, since she won't have me,
A poor fool gone into exile who knows where.

Tristan, no more of me you'll hear,
A poor fool gone into exile who knows where.
I quit singing and give up song
And say to joy and love "so long".

BERNART DE VENTADORN

Translated from Provençal by Geoffrey O'Brien

"It has gone with me as with a child"

It has gone with me as with a child
that saw its beautiful image in a mirror
and reached for its own reflection so
often till it broke the mirror to pieces;
then its contentment turned into a great unrest.
So I, once, thought I would live in continual joy
when I set my eyes on my beloved lady,
through whom, beside some pleasure, I have felt much pain.

Minne, who increases men's joy—look,
there, she brought me my lady by way of a dream,
where my body was turned toward sleep,
lost in the vision of its great contentment.
Then I gazed on all her nobleness, her shining image,
beautiful, exalted among women. Only,
it was just that there was some damage
to her small red mouth, that always laughed.

It frightened me
to see her small mouth pale, that was so red.
Now for this I have raised up new laments:
my heart stood ready for the grief it knew,

and I found this terror with my eyes—
like that child without experience
who found his own reflection in a spring
and had to love it till he died.

Heaven itself cannot contain
women higher in virtue and mind
than this good lady. I have been brought down,
I must stay far away and cleave to her forever.
O sorrow, how for a moment it could seem
I had reached and won her joyful, noble love.
Now here I stand, just starting out,
my contentment is gone, and my soaring dream.

HEINRICH VON MORUNGEN

Translated from German by Frederick Goldin

from **He finds that Love has beguiled him,
but will trust in his Lady**

Often the day had a most joyful morn
            That bringeth grief at last
      Unto the human heart which deemed all well:
Of a sweet seed the fruit was often born
            That hath a bitter taste:
      Of mine own knowledge, oft it thus befell.
I say it for myself, who, foolishly
            Expectant of all joy,
                  Triumphing undertook
      To love a lady proud and beautiful,

For one poor glance vouchsafed in mirth to me:
        Wherefrom sprang all annoy:
           For, since the day Love shook
My heart, she ever hath been cold and cruel.

Well thought I to possess my joy complete
        When that sweet look of hers
        I felt upon me, amorous and kind:
Now is my hope even underneath my feet.
        And still the arrow stirs
        Within my heart—(oh hurt no skill can bind!)—
Which through mine eyes found entrance cunningly!
        In manner as through glass
           Light pierces from the sun,
        And breaks it not, but wins its way beyond,—
As into an unaltered mirror, free
        And still, some shape may pass.
           Yet has my heart begun
        To break, methinks, for I on death grow fond. . . .

And since, in hope of mercy, I have bent
        Unto her ordinance
        Humbly my heart, my body, and my life,
Giving her perfect power acknowledgement,—
        I think some kinder glance
        She'll deign, and, in mere pity, pause from strife.
She surely shall enact the good lord's part:
        When one whom force compels
           Doth yield, he is pacified,
        Forgiving him therein where he did err.

Ah! well I know she hath the noble heart
    Which in the lion quells
      Obduracy of pride;
   Whose nobleness is for a crown on her.

SIMBUONO GIUDICE

Translated from Italian by Dante Gabriel Rossetti

"My lady carries love within her eyes"

My lady carries love within her eyes;
   All that she looks on is made pleasanter;
   Upon her path men turn to gaze at her;
He whom she greeteth feels his heart to rise,
And droops his troubled visage, full of sighs,
   And of his evil heart is then aware:
   Hate loves, and pride becomes a worshipper.
O women, help to praise her in somewise.
Humbleness, and the hope that hopeth well,
   By speech of hers into the mind are brought,
     And who beholds is blessèd oftenwhiles.
    The look she hath when she a little smiles
   Cannot be said, nor holden in the thought;
'Tis such a new and gracious miracle.

DANTE ALIGHIERI

Translated from Italian by Dante Gabriel Rossetti

the Green-Eyed Monster

JEALOUSY HAD A special role in courtly poetry. Its malign appearance was a sure signal that joy, youth, spring, and love—attributes highly prized in courtly love—were nearby. Such tales and poems of jealousy never failed to evoke the generative powers of love.

❀ One speaks of his Feigned and Real Love
    Anonymous (dates unknown)

❀ "Lords, counsel me now"
    Bernart de Ventadorn (1148-1195)

❀ THE DECAMERON: FOURTH DAY, NINTH STORY
    Giovanni Boccaccio (1313-1375)

❀ Rondel to his Mistress
    Charles d'Orléans (1391-1465)

❀ SIR GARNISH OF THE MOUNT
    From *Le Morte D'Arthur* by Sir Thomas Malory (d. 1471)

One speaks of his Feigned and Real Love

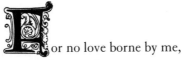or no love borne by me,
Neither because I care
To find that thou art fair,—
To give another pain I gaze on thee.
And now, lest such as thought that thou couldst move
My heart, should read this verse,
I will say here, another has my love.
An angel of the spheres
She seems, and I am hers;
Who has more gentleness
And owns a fairer face
Than any woman else,—at least, to me.

Sweeter than any, more in all at ease,
Lighter and lovelier.
Not to disparage thee; for whoso sees
May like thee more than her.
This vest will one prefer
And one another vest.
To me she seems the best,
And I am hers, and let what will be, be

For no love borne by me,
Neither because I care
To find that thou art fair,—
To give another pain, I gaze on thee.

ANONYMOUS

Translated from Italian by Dante Gabriel Rossetti

"Lords, counsel me now"

Lords, counsel me now,
you who have experience and understanding:
a lady I have long loved
gave me her love;
but now I know beyond all doubt
she keeps another lover close,
and never yet has a companion's
companionship been so hard to bear.

One thing torments me
and makes me pause for thought:
if I acquiesce in this little arrangement
I just prolong my suffering,
but if I tell her exactly what I think,
I see myself with a double loss.
Thus no matter what I do, or don't do,
I can't do myself any good.

And if I love her in dishonor,
I shall be a man whom everyone scorns,
nearly all these people will take me for a cuckold,
a man who really doesn't mind his horns.
But, on the other hand, if I lose her friendship,
I hold myself disowned
by love, and then God never let me
write a *vers* or *canson* again.

Since I am involved in madness,
I would really be mad if I did not choose
of these two evils the lesser one;
for it is better—I see it clearly now—

to have a half of her
than lose her altogether by my raging,
for I never saw a lover full of rancor
do himself any good in love.

Since she wants another lover,
my lady, well, I won't say anything against it,
and I go along with it more from fear
than by choice;
and if ever a man deserved gratitude
for some involuntary service,
then I should have some reward,
I who pardon so great a wrong.

Her beautiful traitor eyes
that once looked on me with much gentleness,
if they look like that elsewhere
they do wrong, great wrong;
yes, but they have done me this great honor:
when a thousand people were gathered together,
there—they look to where I am
more than to all the others around.

With the water I weep from my eyes
I write more than a hundred love letters
and send them to the most beautiful,
the courtliest.
Many times it reminds me afterwards
of what she did when we parted:
I saw her cover her face,
so that she could not tell me yes or no.

Lady, in public love
the other one, and me in private,
so that I get all the good of it,
and he the edifying conversation.

Garsio, now sing my song
for me, and take it
to my Messenger, who was there.
I ask what counsel he would give.

BERNART DE VENTADORN

Translated from Provençal by Frederick Goldin

the decameron: fourth day, ninth story

HERE WERE AFORETIME IN PROVENÇE two noble knights, each of whom had castles and vassals under him, the one called Sir Guillaume de Roussillon and the other Sir Guillaume de Guardestaing. They were both men of great prowess in arms, and they loved each other with an exceeding love. Often they were wont to clad themselves in the same colors at every tournament or jousting or other act of arms.

Although they abode each in his own castle and were distant, one from the other a good ten miles, it came to pass that Sir Guillaume de Roussillon found a very fair and lovesome lady to wife that Sir Guillaume de Guardestaing, without affecting the fellowship between them, became beyond measure enamored of her.

So by various means, the lady became aware of his passion, and knowing him for a very valiant knight, it pleased her very much to return his love. This lovesome lady soon desired nothing more than to tender him or to be solicited by him; both of which was not long in coming to pass as they encountered one another once and many times.

Loving each other thus and conversing together less discreetly than need be, it happened that the husband became aware of the familiarity and was then mightily incensed. The great love he bore unto Guardestaing turned quickly into mortal hatred so that Roussillon was fully resolved to kill him; but this he knew to keep hidden better than the two lovers had known to conceal their love.

Being in this state of mind and hearing that a great tournament was proclaimed in France, Roussillon bid Guardestaing to come to him so they might take counsel together if and how they should go to the games. Hearing this, the other joyously answered that he would without fail come to sup with him on the ensuing day.

Accordingly on the next day, Roussillon armed himself and, mounting his horse with a servant of his, lay at ambush, maybe a mile from his castle, in a wood whereby Guardestaing must pass.

There, after he had awaited him a good while, he saw him come, unarmed and followed by two servants who mirrored their master's carefree spirit. When he saw him come where he would have him, he rushed out upon him, lance in hand, full of rage and malice, crying, "Traitor, thou art dead!" And plunging the lance into his breast, he spoke truthfully. Guardestaing, without being able to make any defense or even to say a word, fell from his horse, transfixed of the lance, whilst his servants, without waiting to learn who had done the deed, turned their horses' heads, and fled as quickly as they might toward their lord's castle.

Roussillon dismounted and opening the dead man's breast with a knife, with his own hands tore out his heart, which he let wrap in cloth and gave to one of his men to carry. Then, commanding that none should dare make words of the matter, he remounted, it being now night, and returned to his castle.

The lady, who had heard that Guardestaing was to be there that evening for supper, looked for him with the utmost impatience, and seeing him not come, marveled sore and said to her husband, "How is it that Guardestaing is not come?"

"Wife," he answered, "I have had word from him that he cannot be here till tomorrow." This little bit of unexpected news troubled the lady deeply, though she knew not why.

Roussillon then dismounted and, calling the cook, said to him, "Take this wild boar's heart and look thou make a dainty dish with it—the best and most delectable that thou knowest. And when I am at the table, send it to me in a silver porringer." The cook accordingly took the heart and, putting all his art and all his diligence into it, minced it, and seasoned it with a store of rich spices, so that he made of it a very dainty ragout.

When it was time, Sir Guillaume sat down to the table with his wife and the viands came; but he ate little, being hindered in thought for the ill deed he had committed. Then the cook sent him the ragout, which he caused to be set before the lady, feigning himself to be full already.

The lady, who was nowise squeamish, tasted the dish and finding it good, ate it all; which when the knight saw this, he said to her, "Wife, what think you of this dish?"

"In truth, my lord," she answered, "it pleaseth me well."

"So God be mine aid," quoth Roussillon, "I do indeed believe you. Nor do I doubt that though it be dead it had pleaseth thee more alive."

The lady, hearing this, hesitated awhile, then said, "How? What have you made me eat?"

"This that you have eaten," answered the knight, "was in very truth the heart of Sir Guillaume de Guardestaing, whom you, disloyal wife that you are, so loved; and know for certain that it is his very heart, for I tore it from his breast with these hands just before I returned."

Hearing this of him whom she loved more than all else, lost herself more in loathing for him, her husband, than in her loathsome act.

"You have done a deed fit for the base and lowly knight that you are. For if I, unforced by him, made him lord of my love and hath offended you, I should have borne the penalty, not he. But hear me now, I pray to God to forbid that any other meal should ever be such noble meat as the heart of so valiant and courteous a knight and gentleman as Sir Guardestaing!"

Then, rising to her feet, without any manner of hesitation, she let herself fall backward through a window which was behind her and which was exceedingly high above the ground; wherefore she not only died, but was broken to pieces.

Sir Guillaume, seeing this, was sore dismayed and dreading the wrath of the country people and of the Count of Provençe for his foul deed, he saddled his horses and exiled himself from the land unto his dying days.

On the following day when it was known all over the country how this thing had passed, the two bodies were taken up by Guardestaing's people and laid in one sepulchre in the chapel of their lord's castle. Then once being laid to rest, on the sepulchre's stone walls were written verses signifying who were buried there within and the tragic manner and occasion of both their love and death.

GIOVANNI BOCCACCIO

Translated from Italian by John Payne, adapted by the editor

Rondel to his Mistress

Strengthen, my Love, this castle of my heart,
 And with some store of pleasure give me aid,
For Jealousy, with all them of his part,
 Strong siege about the weary tower has laid.
 Nay, if to break his bands thou art afraid,
Too weak to make his cruel force depart,
Strengthen at least this castle of my heart,
 And with some store of pleasure give me aid.
Nay, let not Jealousy, for all his art

Be master, and the tower in ruin laid,
   That still, ah Love! thy gracious rule obeyed.
Advance, and give me succour of thy part;
Strengthen, my Love, this castle of my heart.

CHARLES D'ORLÉANS

Translated from French by Andrew Lang

SIR GARNISH OF THE MOUNT

SO BALIN RODE EIGHT DAYS before he met with adventure. And then at last he came into a fair forest in a valley and was aware of a tower, and there beside he saw a great horse of war tied to a tree. There beside sat a fair knight on the ground who made great mourning. He seemed a likely man and well made.

"God save you, why be ye so heavy? Tell me and I will to my power amend it, if I may," said Balin.

"Sir knight," said he, "thou dost give me great grief, for I was in merry thoughts, but now thou puttest me to more pain."

Balin went a little from him and looked on his horse; then Balin heard him say thus: "Ah, fair lady, why have ye broken thy promise, for thou promisest me to meet me here by noon, and I should curse thee that this sword ye ever gave me, for with this sword I will slay myself," and he then pulled it out. And therewith Balin went unto him and took him by the hand.

"Let go my hand," said the knight, "or else I shall slay thee."

"That shall not be," said Balin, "for I shall promise you my help to get you your lady, if ye will tell me where she is."

"What is your name?" said the knight.

"My name is Balin le Savage."

"Ah, sir, I know you well enough. Ye are the Knight with the Two Swords, and the man of most prowess living."

"What is your name?" said Balin.

"My name is Garnish of the Mount, a poor man's son, but by my prowess and hardiness a duke hath made me knight and gave me lands; his name is Duke Hermel, and his daughter is she that I love, and she me as I deemed."

"How far is she hence?" said Balin.

"But six miles," said the knight.

"Now ride we hence then," said Balin, at which the knight joined him.

So they rode more than a pace, till that they came to a fair castle well walled and ditched. "I will enter into the castle," said Balin, "and look if she be there."

So he went in and searched from chamber to chamber and found her bed, but she was not there. Then Balin looked into a fair little garden, and under a laurel tree he saw her lie upon a quilt of green samite and a knight in her arms, fast holding the other, and then under their heads grass and herbs.

When Balin saw her lie so with the foulest knight that ever he saw, and she a fair lady, then Balin went through all the chambers again, and told the knight how he found her as she had slept fast, and so brought him to the place where she lay fast sleeping.

And when Garnish beheld her so lying, for pure sorrow his mouth and nose burst out a-bleeding, and with his sword he smote off both their heads. Then he made sorrow out of measure, and said, "O Balin, much sorrow hast thou brought unto me, for hadst thou not shown me that sight I would have lost my sorrow."

"Forsooth," said Balin, "I did it to this intent that it should better thy courage, and that ye might see and know her falsehood, and to cause you to leave your love of such a lady; God knoweth I did none other but as I would ye did for me."

"Alas," said Garnish, "now is my sorrow double and that I may not endure, for now have I slain all that I most loved in my life."

And therewith he suddenly rove himself on his own sword unto the hilts. When Balin saw that, he dressed him thenceward, lest folk would say he had slain them; and then he rode forth with much sorrow and trouble at such ill-deeds of jealousy.

from LE MORTE D'ARTHUR by Sir Thomas Malory

Adapted by the editor

Satires & Slurs

SATIRE HAD ITS own peculiar form of poetry, called the sirvante. *The* sirvante *might be leveled at an individual and could assume any of various tones—scorn, irony, accusation, or even triumph. In an era with limited networks of communication, the* sirvante *was a powerful instrument for shaping public opinion.*

✹ "Your lover, Madame Sancha, is"
    Raimon de Miravals (c. 1180-1210)

✹ *Tenzon*
    The Marquis of Malespina (c. 1200) and Rambaud of
    Vaquieras (b. 1155?-d. after 1207)

✹ FROM COMMAS TO CANNONBALLS
    from *The Troubadours* by John Rutherford

✹ "Fine joy brings me great happiness"
    Countess of Dia (born c. 1140)

✹ AT THE FEAST OF BEROLDO, LORD OF BAUX
    from *The Troubadours* by John Rutherford

"Your lover, Madame Sancha, is"

Your lover, Madame Sancha, is
    A very nice young man;
But minding business none of his
    Is not a prudent plan:

I wish him well, and therefore hope
    You'll teach him this to know—
That when a nose a-poking goes,
    It often meets a blow.

Me he assails and takes to task
    About a sordid dame;
But if the crime be hers, I ask
    How mine can be the shame?

If he will couple sorry rhymes,
    A better theme would be—
How Amfos knightly faith forgot,
    And Adalais modesty.

The fiend of folly man and mule
    At times must needs possess;
Nor can we check each frantic fool,
    But castigate them—yes.

Your knight, then, punish, Sancha fair,
    And I'll chastise my "mount;"
I'd whop both man and mule, but spare
    The man on your account.

RAIMON DE MIRAVALS

Translated from Provençal by John Rutherford

Tenzon

The Marquis of Malespina and Rambaud of Vaquieras

They tell me, oh, my Rambaud! and I really think it true,
That your mistress has resumed her wit, and quite discarded you,
Despising, as she ought to do, your canzons and yourself,
And fully meaning never more to yield you love or pelf.
The case is hard for such a bard; but you may shun such shame
By mending note; or if you can't, by choosing lowlier dame.

Yes, it is true, as told to you, a false one is my fair,
You ought to wed her, on my word! you'd make a pretty pair!
Unscrupulous are you as she, greedy and treach'rous both,
Still ready, when your interest calls, to break or word or oath.
Nay worse than that, my noble peer, do not the Lombards say
That purses, like a common thief, you took on the highway?

And if I took a purse or two, what's that to you, my friend?
I took them boldly, like a man, and had the heart to spend;
So would I now, if there were need, nor ever shroud my head,
Rather than trudge afoot and beg, as you have done, for bread.
For begging, or for sordidness, there's none that can me blame,
Come, if you can, put hand on heart, and say the very same!

Yes, Marquis, I admit that you are quite a worthy lad,
To cutting purse and breaking oath some virtues more you
add.
Your tongue is quick when one's away, and slow when one's
in sight.
Your spur is sluggish in the charge and eager in the flight.
I know not from what ancestor your nature you inherit,
You're always first in evil deeds and last in works of merit.

Why did you drop the jongleur's harp, the knightly lance to rear?
It was a folly; but a fool, you know, you always were.
That was a jolly life to lead, brimful of freak and fun;
But now you must live soberly and into perils run.
Tho' I must say who on the field have kept you well in sight,
That any day you'd run away, rather than stand and fight.

THE MARQUIS OF MALESPINA AND
RAMBAUD OF VAQUIERAS
Translated from Provençal by John Rutherford

from commas to cannonballs

O IT HAPPENED THAT IN the course of the Hughes of St. Cyr's wanderings through the regions of Provençe he decided to pay a visit to the Count of Rhodez. He was looking for a patron to support himself and his music, and as the baron had formerly granted him a generous pension he didn't think his request would meet much resistance. Unfortunately for the poet though, the Count received him coldly. He even failed to inquire on Hughes's recent health.

Hurt and rejected, the poet retired to a neighboring chateau, where he composed the following lay—despatching it, of course, to the Count the moment he could find a suitable messenger. The messenger, it may be said, was a singer of the lowest class, one of those who made a living singing someone else's song before the composer's subject:

Don't be afraid of my mettlesome blade
Nor raise your eyebrows nor straighten your leg—
I assure you I have not come to beg.
Of this world's goods I have all I need—

As for yourself if you're short of pelf—
    For so it may be
That times have changed with you as with me—
    I do not object my pockets to rifle
    In order to hand your countship a trifle;
I verily think it would be a good deed!

    To this piece of cool impudence the Count, who was also a poet,
replied, and at once, by the same messenger:

You wretched scamp! You inveterate tramp!
Do you indeed forget, or no,
Entering my castle some years ago
Naked without and empty within—
A very scarecrow ragged and thin?
To fatten you up and set you to rights
Cost me more than the board of a couple of knights,
Including their tail of archers and squires—
And now—by the souls of all my sires!
    Those who hear I know will believe—
You inveterate screw! You dare to sue!
If I were to offer a palfrew or two,
By God, you're just the creep to receive!

    Yet the Count, not satisfied with this elegant retort, summoned
his neighbor to expel the troubadour Hughes forthwith. But to this
directive his neighbor refused in a biting song, in whose composition the wandering poet most likely had a share. Thus, the affair
soon devolved into one of those hapless feuds where words turned
to swords, dashes to javelins, and commas to cannonballs.

from THE TROUBADOURS by John Rutherford
Adapted by the editor

"Fine joy brings me great happiness"

Fine joy brings me great happiness,
which makes me sing more gaily,
and it doesn't bother me a bit
or weigh my spirit down
that those sneaky *lauzengiers**   *spies
are out to do me harm;
their evil talk doesn't dismay me,
it just makes me twice as gay.

Those nasty-worded *lauzengiers*
won't get an ounce of trust from me,
for no one will find honor
who has anything to do with them.
They are like the cloud that grows
and billows out until
the sun loses its rays:
I have no use for such as them.

And you, gossiping *gelos,**   *jealous husband
don't think I'm going to hang around,
or that joy and youth don't please me:
beware, or grief will bring you low.

COUNTESS OF DIA

Translated from Provençal by Meg Bogin

at the feast of beraldo, lord of baux

IN THE SOUTH OF FRANCE, perhaps the most refined and luxurious quarter of Europe of that time, there was given a splendid feast at the banquet-hall of Beraldo, Lord of Baux and Viscount of Marseilles. This feast was not lacking in anything that might have adorned a banquet during the age of courtly love. The hall was of sufficient proportions, the costumes, magnificent and unequaled, even for a time when fashion far surpassed our own. Of the hundred delicacies arriving from the kitchen, many of these dishes' preparation and names have not been forgotten. And at the close of the feast, spiced wines along with pastries baked in artistic shapes were served, as tumblers and various minstrels performed about the hall.

It was on this closing note that a cry arose from the audience asking for the appearance of Peire Vidal, the masterful musician of Baux. Soon this cry rose to form a chant, and as this chant increased in volume, Vidal, who was dining with all the others, felt himself obliged to obey their call. So he takes a guitar from an attendant, and runs his fingers over the strings. At this sound, all conversation stops, with even the whispers of lovers halting, as all look on Vidal attentively.

Peire Vidal happens to be in a satiric mood, and his song is a succession of hits, which causes not a few of the guests to wince perceptibly. The song progresses, and as it does, it shows the society of Provençe to be somewhat like our own:

I hate who gives a scanty feast,
    The mind where envy rankles,
A brawling monk, a smirking priest,
    And the maid who shows her ankles.

The fool who dotes upon his wife,
    The churl whose wine's diluted,
The puritan with joy at strife
    May these three be well hooted!

Deep shame befall who wears a sword
    He never draws in fight,
And be the huxter's brat abhorred
    Who apes the airs of knight.

Let scorn be hers who weds her groom,
    And his who weds his harlot,
And may the gibbet be the doom
    Of rogues that strut in scarlet!

Tumultuous applause follows; and, when this subsides, Vidal condescends to entertain the company with his latest song. It is founded on the perilous position of the Christian kingdom in Palestine in the year 1187, just before the news of the capture of Jerusalem by the Saracens arrived to startle the Western world; and it is composed in reprehension of the indifference with which the European Powers regard the crisis.

Shame on the sensual German, too drunk to hear the call
That rings for help across the wave, from Salem's leaguered
        wall!
Shame on the Flemish burghers, a dull and sordid race,
Who play the shuttle while the Turk defiles each holy place!
Shame on the island princes, who waste in sinful fray
The blood and gold that might have swept the pagan from his
        prey!

Shame on the Butcher's offspring, the laggard in the fight,
Who aims to do his neighbor wrong, but not his faith to right.

Shame on the ancient dotard who only tells his beads,
While Saladin a mighty host against King Baldwin leads.
And shame on every singer whose verses will not aid
To rouse the chiefs of Christendom unto a new Crusade.

This piece excites unqualified enthusiasm, and the applause is re-newed in thunderous form. Nor is the audience content with ap-plauding. One throws a gold chain around the poet's neck; another forces a ring on his finger; a third clasps his embroidered sword-belt around his waist; and a fourth casts his mantle over his shoulders.

Yet, as it was generally understood among the people of the time that these gifts were largely symbolic, after the feast these presents bestowed upon Vidal are either reclaimed by their donators or given to a site of Christian faith.

from THE TROUBADOURS by John Rutherford
Adapted by the editor

Chivalry

THOUGH GREATLY DIMINISHED TODAY, the chivalric code, with its basic premise of practicing restraint and courage for love's sake, remains viable. The stories here record a time when chivalry flowered as a new and honorable aspect of the culture and as an innovation in respect for Woman's distinction.

"The envoys of the heart should be"

The envoys of the heart should be
The noble deeds of chivalry:—
A daring charge, an escalade,
A knight or banner captive made;
A pass against a host maintained,
A name through trials borne unstained—
Thus love most eloquently speaks;
This is the homage maiden seeks.

GIRAUD CALANSON

Translated from Provençal by John Rutherford

"Sung in song and told in story"

Sung in song and told in story
Are your triumphs and your glory;
How before you rivals fly,
How around you lovers die!
If you thus resistless be,
You are just the foe for me!
Furbish up your arms anew—
    Weave your wiles,
    Whet your smiles,
    Marshal all your charms like lances,
    Light the Greek fire of your glances—
Spite of all, I'll conquer you.
How? why just as lady bright

Should be vanquished by good knight,
Who in serving best does war her—
Conquering her by conquering for her.
Here am I, with fearless hand—
 Lances lifted, casques on head,
 Coursers bridled, banners spread—
Prompt to ride at your command!
Say what castle shall I win?
 It, be sure,
 I'll secure,
And your heart, as well, within.

SAVARI DE MAULEON

Translated from Provençal by John Rutherford

KING ARTHUR'S YOUNG SQUIRE

KING ARTHUR'S SISTER, MORGAUSE, the Queen of Lothian and Orkney, sat at home in her now lonely castle. As her husband had been killed in battle with King Pellinore, she had sent her children off at an early age to her brother's service where their energy could take root and flourish nobly. The youngest of her sons, Gareth, a tall, sturdy lad, was the last to leave Lothian. He heard tales of his brothers' prowess and their honorable acts in the service of his uncle, so he was anxious to meet up with the Knights of the Round Table and prove himself a worthy knight as well.

Now as the young man neared the castle in the country of Wales, where the king was holding his feast of Whitsuntide, Gareth decided to take the hard, perilous route for making a name for himself. He was going to make himself known through his acts, as the thought of resting on his family's heritage for recognition only cheapened his spirit. So Gareth put aside all his marks of rank and nobility and exchanged them for some servant's clothes. Thus dressed, so that not even his three older brothers recognized him, he entered King Arthur's court, serving fine victuals and drink.

And for twelve months, he lived the hard, difficult life of the servant, with only his days off providing him pleasure of watching the games and trials of strength amongst the brave knights. When Whitsuntide rolled around again, he again played servant. But this time Arthur's feast would have an uninvited guest who from henceforth would change Gareth's life.

As the feast was just beginning, a young woman, worn and disheveled from her long travel to Wales, walked into the hall and kneeled before King Arthur, piteously seeking his aid. Her name was Linet and she was from the court of the Lady of Lyonnesse. A cruel tyrant, Sir Ironside, or the Red Knight as many knew him, had been wasting away her Lady's lands and besieging her Lady's castle for the past two years, taking his toll on a kingdom whose Lord had just passed away of illness.

Now before anyone had answered the lady's plea, Gareth came pushing through the crowd, crying out, "King, heaven thank you! For twelve months I have lived here as I desired, and now let me ask just this one request. Grant me nothing else, but your approval to free this lady from the Red Knight's power."

Stunned at this plea, the crowd in Arthur's court fell silent, but Arthur's eyes delighted before this act of wild ambition for such a noble cause. So when he gestured to the young man in approval, it seemed to all watching as if he was answering from his heart.

"So be it," he said. "This adventure shall be yours, Gareth, for I am sure you will prove right and worthy for this most noble deed."

Now Linet didn't realize that King Arthur had been watching the young servant closely for the past twelve months. More than once, Gareth had emerged victorious from the various contests held amongst Arthur's servants and pages. Though unaware of his birthright, he knew Gareth's vigor and strength could challenge any experienced knight. But insulted to be given such a poor ranking champion for her town and Lady, Linet turned, and without another word, mounted her horse and sped away.

Soon she was a good distance off, so Gareth looked to King Arthur as to what to do next. Arthur gave him then a horse, arms, and his blessings. With these gifts, Gareth set off, and as his horse was freshly rested and bathed, he had little trouble catching up to the fleeing Linet.

Though she now saw him horsed and armed like a knight, she was still unimpressed. And as he neared, she cursed him.

"What are you doing here, ladle washer! Your clothes look foul with grease and tallow! How can you help me? You knave! Go and fight your soup flies! You kitchen swill!"

So in this manner they continued, until they came to a dark section of the forest where stood a knight dressed in black armor beside a black horse and holding a black shield. He held this passage against all comers, so read his banner.

"Now this should turn him back," thought the young Linet. "Never would he venture against such a knight."

But Gareth was determined. He asked the knight for passage so that he might free the town of Lyonnesse from its tyrant, but the Black Knight laughed at this request, and putting his lance in position replied: "Let's see what thou can do against this!"

Then wrathfully both knights spurred their horses and rode at one another, while the damsel rode on, not bothering to look back on the battle starting. At the first shock, the Black Knight's spear splintered against Gareth's shield, but Gareth sat firm, and his spear pierced through the other's side and broke off, leaving the point still in his body. Nevertheless the Black Knight drew his sword and smote fiercely, and gave Gareth many sore strokes. But his wound weakened the Black Knight, and his blows became wilder and fainter, and suddenly he fell off his horse in a swoon.

Gareth then seeing his opponent down; unmounted and removed the Knight's arms, and then rode after the damsel, hoping now for a kinder greeting. But this he did not receive.

"Away!" she cried, as he drew near. "There are two more knights on this road to Lyonnesse, friends of the knight you have just tricked of his arms. Leave and get out of here now before they make you pay dearly for what you've done."

And in riding with Linet, Gareth then encountered both the Blue and Green Knights as she mentioned, and slew them both.

Then catching up to her a fourth time, Gareth said: "Look! I will not leave your side no matter what you say. Just lead me to your troubled town and Lady. This is my adventure that I've undertaken and I'll either succeed or die because of it."

"I wonder," cried Linet, "what kind of man you might be. You prove worthy of some merit. Nevertheless, the Red Knight is seven times as strong as those other knights you've encountered. I worry what could become of you."

No longer content with his secret, Gareth then told her everything of his noble upbringing and success in Arthur's court. This truth and his overcoming the three knights finally quieted her greatest doubts, so that the two of them approached Lyonnesse in good spirits.

Now on approaching the castle of Lyonnesse, they saw the arms and armor of twenty knights hung and displayed as trophies. This horde of armor Gareth knew to be the spoils of the Red Knight's victories. Yet, still this did not deter him. Beside the armor was the banner of Sir Ironside, and beside the banner was a mighty horn of ivory, which Gareth sounded.

Straight out from the forest rode the Red Knight. He taunted the young man before him. "Who is this that comes to his death, like so many before him?"

Gareth replied, "Who calls himself a knight that takes on a castle whose Lord is no longer."

At this reply, the Red Knight readied his horse as did Gareth at his end of the field and then both galloped straightway together with all their might.

Dreadful was the shock of their encounter! So truly did the spears strike in the midst of either shield that their girths and cruppers burst, and the riders were hurled to the ground with the bridles in their hands. All who saw thought their necks had been broken, but they sprang up and drew their swords and ran at one another. Each gave the other a blow that made him reel backward; then recovering, they closed again in furious fight, hewing, cutting, slashing, clashing, and thrusting till both were out of breath. Now they drew back and leant panting on their swords; then they hurtled together like two fierce lions. At one time they would fall to the earth and wrestle there; at another time, in the madness of the struggle, each would snatch up the other's sword instead of his own. The Red Knight was a wily swordsman and taught Gareth to be wily in turn, but he paid dearly for it with his blood before he could learn that foe's manner of fighting. Yet the young knight, too, dealt many a shrewd stroke at him, and the blood ran down their bodies, and the armor of each was so hewn that in many places men might see their naked sides.

Thus for an hour and more they fought, and none of the beholders could say which of them was likely to win the battle.

So weary grew they that by assent of their exhaustion they paused a while and sat down. But when Gareth's helm was off he looked up to the castle windows, and caught sight of the fair Lady of Lyonnesse, and that gave him heart for the combat, so that he called on the Red Knight to make ready forthwith, and they started up at once and fell to it again with fresh fury, till the ground at their feet was covered with blood and pieces of broken armor.

But at last Gareth's strength began to fail, while the other doubled his strokes and pressed on him more and more sorely. He bore his shield low for weariness, his arm waxed fainter, his foot slipped, and his sword was forced out of his hand. Then with one blow the

Red Knight clove his shield, with another he laid him on the earth, and stood already bending over him to make an end, when Linet was heard aloud:

"Ah! my knight, Where is your courage? Aie! how I cry to see you fall!"

These words brought the youth back to life. With a mighty bound he gained his feet, and nimbly springing to and gripping his own sword, dealt the Red Knight such a blow on the head that he now fell to the earth, and Gareth stooped over him to hold him fast. Then all in the castle shouted for joy.

"Hold your hand," the Red Knight cried, "and hear me out. A lady I loved whose brother was slain by one of the knights of King Arthur sent me out to meet with a Lancelot or Gawain. So to draw them out, I stirred up trouble, but now I see how foul were my deeds. Let me make amends and all my men and myself will have you as our liege and do you homage."

"I am full of loathing," said Gareth, "to slay any knight that does his lady's bidding; and so I will yield your life if the Lady of Lyonnesse forgives you. And then if that is done, you must go to Camelot to make your case with Arthur's court and not with beleaguered lands."

"Sir," said the Red Knight, "all this will I do as you command."

Then painfully Gareth watched him rise. The Red Knight bid his men to bring meat and drink for Gareth, and Sir Ironside himself waited on him courteously. Next came Linet, who unarmed him and staunched his wounds; and then did the same to the Red Knight. And when their hurts were dressed they all went inside the castle to see the fair Lady of Lyonnesse, whom a servant boy had freed.

from LE MORTE D'ARTHUR by Sir Thomas Malory
Retold by A. R. Moncrieff, adapted by the editor

from "**When the ice and the cold and the snow**"

ood lady, this ring of yours,
this ring you gave me helps me greatly:
it sweetens my sorrow
when I gaze on it, I become lighter
than a starling;
and then, because of you, I become so brave
I never fear any arrow or lance
can harm me; no iron or steel can touch me.
A moment later and I am more lost,
through too much loving,
than a ship whirled round by the sea,
pulled apart by waves and winds.
So I am racked with thought.

Lady, like a castle
besieged by powerful lords,
perrier, catapult, and mangonel
knock the towers down,
and war bears down so

heavily, from all directions,
no device, no cunning can help the besieged,
the anguish and the shrieks are tremendous and wild
of those inside, who are in terror,
then you see
they have nothing left but to call out for mercy—
that is how I beg you for mercy, in great humility,
my lady, my good and gentle and kind.

Lady, as a lamb
is powerless against a bear,
so am I, wanting
your strength, weaker than a reed.
And my life will be
briefer than the fourth part of an instant
now if any harm should come my way
and you still deny me justice for all this neglect.
And you, True Love, bear me up,
preserve
true lovers from doing foolish things,
be my guide and witness
with my lady, see now how she conquers me.

GIRAUT DE BORNELH

Translated from Provençal by Frederick Goldin

lancelot, knight of the cart

PON A CERTAIN ASCENSION DAY, King Arthur held a very magnificent feast at Camelot. The feast had just ended when there came into the court a knight, fully armed. He gave no greeting but spoke out, "King Arthur, I hold in captivity knights, ladies, and damsels who belong to thy land, and I come to tell you that you have neither the strength nor the resources to free them and return them back to your lands."

The King admitted that he had to endure what he could not change; yet still he was filled with much grief. Hearing this, the knight departed from the hall, but just before he was to pass through the doorway, he turned around and said to King Arthur, "King, if there is a single knight in whom you would entrust to accompany the Queen to meet me in the forest where I am going, I will await him, and if he is able to return the Queen to you after I have met him in combat, I will release all your people to you." He then proceeded to leave the hall completely.

Now Sir Kay, who had just started eating, got up from his seat and said to King Arthur that he was leaving Camelot never to return. The King was very displeased and asked if there was anything he might do to persuade him to stay. After many refusals on the part of Sir Kay and many pleas from King Arthur, Kay finally yielded saying that if the King will grant him the favor he is about to ask, then will he remain with the court. The King granted him his wish, so Sir Kay then asked to accompany the Queen out to the woods where he might then encounter the knight that was holding many of King Arthur's people hostage.

The court was alarmed, and all thought Sir Kay's request outrageous, proud, and mad. Yet the King felt it his duty to keep his word, though it has made both him and his Queen very sorry. Nevertheless, he gave Sir Kay complete charge of the Queen.

As he prepared his arms and horse to encounter the knight, the Queen began to mount her palfrey, sighing to herself, "If you only knew it, I am sure you would never allow me to be led away." Count Guinable, who was standing nearby, overheard her and grew worried about that which was soon to pass.

When the two had finished their preparations, they left the castle and a great lament filled all those present. Now Sir Gawain witnessed this scene and said to the King, "Sir, you are foolish to allow Sir Kay to challenge this knight alone. As they are still nearby, let us follow him, and all others who wish to accompany us." King Arthur agreed, so all involved readied their horses and arms and set out.

As they neared the forest, they saw Kay's horse running out wildly, its stirrups and saddle stained with blood. They then spotted Sir Kay severely injured. All in the group were chagrined at this, and they nudged and shook their heads.

Now Gawain, holding onto Sir Kay's horse, was riding in front of the party, so he was the first to see a knight on a horse that was sore and painfully tired. Gawain recognized this knight as Sir Lancelot, who spoke to him thus: "You see my horse is in a sweat and no longer serviceable. Now with the understanding that I shall return the service and the favor, I beg you to let me have one of your two horses, either as a loan or outright as a gift." So Gawain replied, "Choose whichever one you prefer." Lancelot did not try to select the better of the horses, but leaped quickly upon the one which was nearer to him and rode off. The horse that Sir Lancelot had left behind then fell dead for the knight had ridden him hard that day.

Sir Gawain then followed Sir Lancelot through the forest until he came to the bottom of a hill where he saw the horse that he had just given away dead and the ground strewn with broken shields and lances and trampled by horses. It seemed to him that a great combat had taken place between many knights, and Gawain was very sorry to have missed it.

So Gawain continued on. He then saw Lancelot alone on foot, almost completely armed. He had overtaken a cart. In those days carts were not used as frequently as they are now. In every good town there are three thousand such carts now whereas in those times there was only one. This one cart was used in the town to carry murderers or traitors or thieves. The convicted criminal was put on the cart and then carried through the streets, abused by the people, and thenceforth lost all his legal rights. He was never afterward heard, honored, or welcomed in any court. Such carts were so dreadful in those days that there was a saying, "When thou dost see and meet a cart, cross thyself and call upon God, that no evil may befall thee."

Sir Lancelot on foot, and without a lance, walked behind the cart and saw a dwarf sitting on the shafts. Then he cried out, "Dwarf, for God's sake, tell me now if thou has seen my lady, the Queen, pass by here." The miserable, low-born dwarf would not give him any news of her, but replied, "If thou wilt get up into the cart I am driving thou shalt hear tomorrow what has happened to the Queen." Then the dwarf kept on his way without giving him further heed. Sir Lancelot then hesitated. For common sense, which is inconsistent with love's dictates, bid him refrain from getting in, warning him and counseling him to undertake nothing for which he may reap shame and disgrace. Reason, which dared thus speak to him, reached only his lips, but not his heart; for love was enclosed within his heart, bidding him and urging him to mount at once upon the cart. So he jumped in, since love will have it so, feeling no concern about the shame, since he was prompted by love's commands.

Soon Lancelot, riding in the cart driven by the dwarf, was joined again by Gawain who chose to remain on his horse. So the three journeyed to a very rich and beautiful town. They all entered through the main gate, where the people were startled to see the knight riding upon the cart. The small and great; the old and young; the men and women shouted taunts at him in the streets, and threatened him with many vile and scornful words.

The dwarf then drove the cart to a tower. There the two knights were provided shelter and a meal by a damsel and two charming maidens, while the dwarf quietly withdrew, never to be seen again. After overcoming some obstacles that night, the next morning found the two knights and damsel looking out over the nearby meadows from a high window in the tower. From there they see a bier holding a knight with three maidens in mourning followed by a group of people being led by a knight who was escorting Queen Guenever. Lancelot, sorry for not being near his Queen, wanted to throw himself out the window, but Gawain successfully restrained him. The damsel of the tower taunted him again about riding in the cart and made many jokes of the matter, but when the two knights decided to leave, she courteously treated Lancelot to a new horse and lance as a token of good will.

So the two knights left the tower but were unable to overtake the procession, which was moving rapidly. They continued through the woods along a beaten road when they encountered another damsel. Anxious to recover the Queen, they asked her if she had seen the procession recently. Surprisingly she replied with a full description of the Queen's recent travails.

"My lords," she began, "Meleagant, a tall and powerful knight, son of Bagdemagus, the King of Gore, has taken her off into the kingdom where no foreigner returns. It is possible to enter this land only through two perilous paths. One is called the 'water-bridge' that has the same amount of water above the bridge as below it and is only a foot-and-a-half wide. There are also a number of other obstacles related with this bridge, but of those I will say nothing. The other more perilous route is through the 'sword-bridge,' which is shaped just like a sharp sword and has never been passed over by any man."

She then showed the two knights the two roads leading toward the two bridges. Lancelot, the Knight of the Cart, decided to take the more perilous, but closer, "sword-bridge" path, while Gawain would take the "water-bridge." Having decided this matter, the two knights thanked the maiden and then made their separate departures down the two roads.

Therein follows the adventures of the Knight of the Cart: of how he overcame a knight guarding a ford with a damsel; of how he bravely defended a woman who wished to lie with him though he greatly desired to lie in bed alone; of how he found the comb of Queen Guenever with many strands of her hair tangled therein and treasured her tresses beyond all wealth and herbal medicines; of how he lifted the stone lid of an enormous sarcophagus whose inscription prophesied the liberation of the people of Logres by whomever can lift its stone lid, which took seven men to put in place; of how he defeated many assailants along "the stony passage"; of how word of his deeds and mission spread and incited the captive folk to revolt; and finally of how he crossed the "sword-bridge" and forced the capitulation of King Bagdemagus and the liberation of the Queen and his people.

Yet throughout all these adventures he did receive much abuse and anger from his own people for his one short ride in the cart. But for all this abuse, nothing caused him greater sorrow and grief than Queen Guenever's rejection of him upon his victory. Indeed, the cold shoulder from the Queen and its infliction of despair and self-loathing upon him brought him closer to death than any one of his foes.

For it was only his discovery of the cause of his lady's disdain that brought hope and strength into his heart again. He then vehemently cursed his crime of hesitating for a moment to enter the cart and apologized greatly to her. Hearing his words passionately said, she then granted him her pardon, for she saw in his angered curses and pleas Reason removed from his heart and his life's devotion to her revealed. And this cheered her greatly, for though she found herself married to King Arthur, she regarded this Knight of the Cart both secretly and ardently as her knight and lover.

from LANCELOT, KNIGHT OF THE CART by Chrétien de Troyes
Translated from French by W. Wistar Comfort, adapted by the editor

"I want to make half-a-sirventes upon two kings"

I want to make half-a-sirventes upon two kings,
 and we shall see which of the two is more a knight!
 Alfons, the valiant king of Castile, who is en route
 and will want soldiers,
 or Richard

who spends gold and silver by the gallon and hogshead
and makes all his pleasure in spending and giving,
          refusing all truce,
and seeks war with more heat than a sparrowhawk cast at
  a quail!

If both kings are intrepid and bold, without fail
          we'll see soon
          fields strewn
     with wreckage and quartered corpses, with
       saddle-trees and brackmarts,
          helms and escutcheons,
everywhere corpses split through like kindling
          from the head to the fly,
             and destriers on every side
                running at random,
                   and many long lances stuck through
                      broadsides and chests,
witnesses
of great joy and tears, great distress and wild glee,
great will the hurt be, but the gain greater!

Horns, drums, standards, pennons and oriflammes, horses
black and white
that's what we'll see soon!
And it'll be good living then
liberating what the usurer owns.

By God, there won't be one safe packhorse on the roads,
     we'll make the bourgeois shiver!
Merchants won't get away anymore, walking the roads in
  peace,
the damned costermongers, the route to France at least,
and every man is rich who'll just up and plunder.

And if I see the king, I have faith in God I'll
either come off living, or by the sword and lance,
I'll come off in quarters!

And if I come off living, it'll mean great riches,
and if I die—a great deliverance.

BERTRAN DE BORN

Translated from Provençal by Paul Blackburn

Cult of Youth & Spring

THOUGH THE CHURCH assumed both political and spiritual reign in the courtly era, parades and rites of spring, pagan in origin, still remained popular among the people. Glad to have a means for attracting a larger audience, the troubadours early on adapted the elements of this primitive magic into their songs. For May was a time of free courtship, and June a favorite month for marriage.

❦ "In April when the flowers spring"
    Heinrich von Veldeke (late 12th century)

❦ "The wind is fair"
    Arnaut de Mareuil (late 12th century)

❦ May
    Folgore da San Geminiano (c. 1270-c. 1330)

❦ *from* "Would you like to hear the *muse* of Muset?"
    Colin Muset (early 13th century)

❦ *from* "I thrive on youth and joy"
    Countess of Dia (born c. 1140)

"In April when the flowers spring"

In April when the flowers spring,
the lindens leaf out, the beeches turn green,
with a will the birds begin to sing,
for they all find love where they seek it,
in their mates, so their joy is great—
which I never minded, for all winter long they keep still.

When they saw on the branches the blossoms
springing among the leaves, then they were rich
in the varied songs they always sang.
They started to sing joyfully and loud,
low and high. My mind, too, is such
that I want to know joy. I ought to praise my luck.

If I could win my lady's grace,
could seek it as becomes her!
I shall die, and it will be my fault
unless she consents to accept
a penance other than death for her grace; and so it must be,
for God never commanded any man be glad to die.

HEINRICH VON VELDEKE

Translated from German by Frederick Goldin

"The wind is fair"

The wind is fair
that flows upon me
late in April before May starts up.
And nightingale and jay sing
                against the crickets
                the whole peaceful night.
Each bird announces his joy without restraint
                in his own language
                in the morning freshness
settles down with his mate.

All earthly things rejoice the birth of leaves:
nor can I help remembering the love in which
                I rejoice.
        By usage and by nature I
                turn toward joy
                like any other single creature;
                there where the soft wind blows
                my heart goes,
                revives.

Whiter than Helen,
lithe in gracefulness,
more than the fresh-opened flower is fair
                she is fair;
                white teeth,
                true words,
                open-hearted,
                without trickery,
        clear complexion and auburn hair—

O God, who grants her this seignory*, preserve her,   *rank of power
for one more lovely than she is I have never seen.

If she does not prolong the dispute
I shall count myself blessed,
instead were to give me to start with
a kiss,
and so forth,
according to my length of service.
For then
we shall make a short journey often
down a short path,
since her fine body
has set me readily
in this course.

ARNAUT DE MAREUIL

Translated from Provençal by Paul Blackburn

May

I give you horses for your games in May,
    And all of them well-train'd unto the course,—
    Each docile, swift, erect, a goodly horse;
With armor on their chests, and bells at play
Between their brows, and pennons fair and gay;
    Fine nets, and housing meet for warriors,
    Emblazon'd with the shields ye claim for yours,
Gules, argent, or, all dizzy at noonday.
And spears shall split, and fruit go flying up
In merry counterchange for wreaths that drop

From balconies and casements far above;
And tender damsels with young men and youths
Shall kiss together on the cheeks and mouths;
    And every day be glad with joyful love.

FOLGORE DA SAN GEMINIANO

Translated from Italian by Dante Gabriel Rossetti

from "**Would you like to hear the *muse* of Muset?**"

ould you like to hear the *muse* of Muset?
It was made in May one little morning,
in a flowering orchard, all spring-green,
at the time of day
when the little birds sing
from great joy,
and I went to make a chaplet
in the green.
I made it handsome, fine, and elegant,
all full of flowers.
A young lady,
very beautiful and pleasant,
a pretty girl,
with a little smiling mouth,
called me back:
"Come here, fiddle
. . . .
your *muse* while you so
sweetly sing."

I went to her in the little field
with fiddle and bow
and sang her my *muset*
with great love:
"I have put my heart in a heart so good,
aflame with love . . ."

And when I saw her blond head
and her color
and her sweet body with all that love in it,
and so decked out,
my heart leaps up
for that girl;
my joy keeps on
starting up again.
She had on a tunic
of cloth from Castile
that shimmers.
Sweet God, I love her so
with a heart that keep faith.

When I had fiddled to her
for her love and pleasure,
she rewarded me well,
she was kind,
with a kiss that I wanted.
God, how I love her!
And another thing she gave me,
gave me as her friend,
that I had much desired:
now my wages are paid.

I have more joy
than I was ever used to,
for the one I desire
is mine. . . .

COLIN MUSET

Translated from French by Frederick Goldin

from "I thrive on youth and joy"

I thrive on youth and joy,
and youth and joy keep me alive,
for my friend's the very gayest,
which makes me gay and playful;
and since I'm true,
he should be faithful:
my love for him has never strayed,
nor is my heart the straying kind.

I'm very happy, for the man
whose love I seek's so fine.
May God with joy richly repay
the man who helped us meet.
If anyone should disagree,
pay him no heed; listen only
to the one who knows one often picks the blooms
from which one's own broom's made. . . .

I've picked a fine and noble man,
in whom merit shines and ripens—
generous, upright and wise,
with intelligence and common sense.

I pray him to believe my words
and not let anyone persuade him
that I ever would betray him,
except I found myself betrayed.

Floris, your worth
is known to all good men;
therefore I make this request:
please, grant me your protection. . . .

COUNTESS OF DIA

Translated from Provençal by Meg Bogin

To his Lady, in Spring

o see the green returning
    To stream-side, garden, and meadow,—
To hear the birds give warning,
    (The laughter of sun and shadow
Awakening them full of revel,)
    It puts me in strength to carol
A music measured and level,
    This grief in joy to apparel;
For the deaths of lovers are evil.

Love is a foolish riot,
    And to be loved is a burden;
Who loves and is loved in quiet
    Has all the world for his guerdon.
Ladies on him take pity
    Who for their sake hath trouble:
Yet, if any heart be a city

From love embarrèd double,
Thereof is a joyful ditty.

That heart shall be always joyful;—
    But I in the heart, my lady,
Have jealous doubts unlawful,
    And stubborn pride stands ready.
Yet love is not with a measure,
    But still is willing to suffer
Service at his good pleasure:
    The whole Love hath to offer
Tends to his perfect treasure.

Thine be this prelude-music
    That was of thy commanding;
Thy gaze was not delusive,—
    Of my heart thou hadst understanding.
Lady, by thine attemp'rance
    Thou heldst my life from pining:
This tress thou gav'st, in semblance
    Like gold of the third refining,
Which I do keep for remembrance.

GIACOMINO PUGLIESI, KNIGHT OF PRATO

Translated from Italian by Dante Gabriel Rossetti

the kiss

THE POETS OF the Middle Ages portrayed the pursuit of love as a quest much closer in spirit to a pilgrimage than a crusade. For many, an important part of this spiritual journey was the kiss, which signified a momentous link that could join heaven with earth.

from **"The little birds of my country"**

The little birds of my country
I have heard in Brittany.
When their song rises up, I think
I used to hear them, once,
in sweet Champagne,
if I am not mistaken.
They have put me in such gentle thought,
I have set myself to sing
till I at last attain
what Love has long been promising. . . .

My sweet gentle lady
kissing me stole away my heart;
it was crazy to quit me
for her who torments me.
Alas, I never felt it
leaving me;
she took it so gently,
she drew it to her as I sighed;
she covets my mad heart
but will never have pity for me.

That one kiss, which is always on my mind,
is over, I now realize—
it has betrayed me,
I do not feel it on my lips.
When she permitted,
God! what I am telling of,

why didn't she furnish me against my death.
She knows I am killing myself
in this long expectation,
my face is pale and colorless.

And so she takes away my joy and laughter
and makes me die of longing;
Love makes me pay dearly
again and again for her obligingness.
Alas, I don't dare go to her,
because I have this crazy look
which these false lovers get me blamed for.
I am dead when I see them talking to her there,
because not one of them will find
any of their treachery in her.

GACE BRULÉ

Translated from French by Frederick Goldin

queen isoult's love potion

 O WITH IT AGREED THAT the young Isolt of Ireland would wed the King of Cornwall, King Mark, Tristan asked of Isolt's father, Gurman, to prepare a ship and crew so that he could deliver Isolt to Cornwall in safety, which he so did.

Now while Tristan and Gurman's men were making the ship ready for the voyage, Queen Isoult, Isolt's mother, with much craft and wisdom, prepared a love potion of such power and magic that whoever drank of it would love each other from that moment on, without any will of their own. For so strong did she make that potion that life and death and joy and sorrow could be said to be contained in that little crystal flask.

Then Queen Isoult took the drink and spoke softly to her mistress of the court, Brangoene: "Brangoene, I ask that you go with Isolt as she travels overseas, so now listen carefully: Take this flask with its potent drink within and keep it in your care. Treasure it above all other treasures, and see that no one knows about it and that particularly no one at all drinks from it; but when Isolt and King Mark be joined, then do thou pour it out as wine, and then see they drink of it. Above all forget not this, that this is a mighty love potion—do not tempt to taste it thyself. The life of Isolt, my dearest daughter, and my life as well, doth hang on your care. To be sure, both of us are entrusted to thee on the peril of her eternal welfare."

"My most good lady," said Brangoene, "I will go with Isolt, and watch over her honor and her welfare with all my life."

Then when Tristan and his men made ready the ship, the king and queen and all their household accompanied Isolt to the boat that would take her away. With much weeping, and some smiles of good fortune, the king and queen bid good-bye to their daughter, as did the kinfolk to their men who accompanied Tristan and Isolt in their journey. They pushed from the shore, and with a loud voice all sang, "So sail we forth in the name of God." Thus they departed from Ireland.

Now Isolt was much sore on departing from shore, for she bemoaned herself terribly that she must part from her land where she knew all the folk and from friends who were dear to her. And her journey to an unknown region frightened her much. Though comfort her as much as he did, with kind words and many pledges for her safety, Tristan failed to thoroughly quell her sorrow and fears. So needing respite from the sea though they traveled not far, Tristan pulled the ship ashore near pleasant land, fastened it well, and then there they rested. But Isolt and a few of her maidens remained aboard. Tristan then went into the cabin to greet his liege lady, and sat down beside her, and the two spoke of this thing and of that, till Tristan became thirsty and bid one of the maidens to bring a drink.

One of Isolt's maidens, finding the flask where Brangoene had laid it, said, "See, here is wine in a flask." So she took the flask from its hiding place and brought it to Tristan, and then he gave the drink to Isolt. She poured the drink, thinking it was wine, into a cup, drank of it, and then passed the cup to Tristan, who then partook of the drink as well.

It so happened that just after Tristan finished the drink, Brangoene entered the cabin, and seeing what happened, turned white with terror. Cold at heart and numb in the limbs, she grabbed both the cup and the crystal flask and flung them out to sea.

"Aie! miserable woman that I am," she said to herself, "Curse the day my fate was made. My honor is lost and all my doings a failure. Would to God I had never come on this journey. Better that I had fallen dead than to have given myself to sail with Isolt on this cursed voyage. O Tristan and Isolt! that drink shall be your death."

Once the love potion entered Tristan and Isolt, the ingredients opened therein and laid waste to what ill will may have passed between them. No longer did Isolt fear Tristan for being her protector in this voyage nor did she feel great hatred of him for slaying her uncle; and the anger of Tristan at her cowardliness and unforgiving ways passed quickly as well. Love then, the great mover, met with no resistance in joining the two, and planting his banner of conquest over them brought them easily under his rule. Their hearts now cleansed of hatred and spite became excited and thrilled at their new state of pureness. So much so did their hearts open up to each other that only in one another did they see the promise of true freedom revealed. But then their eyes opened and espying the poor, dying world about them, they painfully realized that only her for him and him for her would do, so that their freedom quickly became bonds and their bonds iron chains. They fought and struggled hard against all these perceptions, but when they denied their hearts their eyes would give testament, and if they darkened their sight, their hearts so pure and powerful burned away at what held back their eyes from seeing.

So enraptured were they by this pell-mell of sensations for love of one another that neither dared to express it to the other for great dread of rejection and of turning their joy to despair. For so ever how long great Love ruled within them, they held between them their honor, so great was their love for their homelands. For Isolt's honor was to fulfill the promises of her parents, King and Queen of Ireland, and for Tristan his duty of bringing Isolt to his uncle, King Mark, King of Cornwall. And the peace and well-being of both countries depended on the success of their mission. So while they felt the pangs of Love and his sting strike deep, neither one approached the other. Tristan motioned toward her but it was only a thought, the desire of his fancy, for in truth, he desired to halt his desires, and did so. Yet when he looked up at Isolt, he felt the pain of love grow stronger, so that soon he knew of no other pain. And when he turned away from her and looked into his own heart, all he saw was Love and Isolt. So that the great debate was quieting in him, and soon he would be ready to give his hand unto Love to lead and guide him without question.

With Isolt as well, she struggled against the tide and fought the waves of sensation rolling over her, yet the more she strove, the more her tired limbs wished to let themselves float and be carried away by the tides. She would look upon Tristan, but only to have shame avert her eyes. So then did Love and Shame make great battle within her till her body could take no more of this strife, this fruitless tearing away at her body and soul. The exhaustion from not loving him and loving him grew great and wearisome, so soon she knew she would have to yield to this new youthful power wrought inside her.

Shyly she looked on him, and he on her, till their hearts and eyes joined and commingled. And Love who could turn sweet sour or sour sweet, turned his artistry unto Isolt and Tristan, turning them from white to red and then from red to white as they looked at each other, much like an artist pleased to see the sun make various shades on a mountain. Thus were they both vanquished by Love. And resigned to defeat, they then made talk of little things. Tristan told Isolt of a previous journey to Ireland when he taught Queen Isoult how to play the lute, and how she mistook him at first for the minstrel Tantris. Yet despite such talk, Isolt grew sad.

"Isolt," he said, "why look so troubled? Why the sorrow?"

"What I know troubles me; what I see brings me sorrow. The sky and sea weary me, and life seemeth to weigh heavy on me."

She stirred a little and then leaned against him, finding his shoulders for support. Then Tristan, seeing her head bent down and her lips flush red with sorrow, laid his arm around her gently, and spoke softly, "Ah, why so troubled? What ails thee?"

And Isolt spoke in riddle: "*L'Amer*," she said, "doth trouble me, it weighs down my soul and bringeth me sorrow."

Then Tristan took note of her words, and saw the double meanings of what she said. For *L'Amer* could be the sea as well as love, but of the latter he would say nothing, so instead he said: "I guess, fair Isolt, that the sea and the wind troubleth thee; and sea, and the salt sea wind; thou dost taste them, and they are alike bitter to thee."

"Nay, what sayest thou? I taste nor wind nor sea. *L'Amer* alone doth trouble me."

And Tristan whispered, "Of a sooth, sweetheart, so doth it me. *L'Amer* and thou, ye are my sorrow! Heart's lady, sweet Isolt, thou and the love of thee have turned my heart asunder; so far have I wandered that nevermore may I find the right path. All that mine eyes behold is but weariness and sorrow, weakness of spirit and heaviness of heart; in all the world is there nought that my heart doth love save thee only."

"Even so is it with me," Isolt said.

So the two made their confession of love each to the other; he kissed her, and she him; and each drank of the sweetness that the heart may offer. Yet they kept the matter secret, that none in the world might know their hearts' desire. 'Twas enough that each knew the will of the other.

from TRISTAN AND ISOLT by Gottfried von Strassburg
Translated from German by Jessie Weston, adapted by the editor

from **"Sweet cries and cracks"**

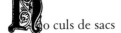o culs de sacs
        nor false ways me deflected
When first I pierced her fort within its dykes,
Hers, for whom my hungry insistency
Passes the gnaw whereby was Vivien wracked;
Day-long I stretch, all times, like a bird preening,
And yawn for her, who hath o'er others thrust her
As high as true joy is o'er ire and rages.

Welcome not lax,
        and my words were protected
Not blabbed to other, when I set my likes
On her. Not brass but gold was 'neath the die.
That day we kissed, and after it she flacked
O'er me her cloak of indigo, for screening
Me from all culvertz' eyes, whose blathered bluster
Can set such spites abroad; win jibes for wages.

God who did tax
        not Longus' sin, respected
That blind centurion beneath the spikes
And him forgave, grant that we two shall lie

Within one room, and seal therein our pact,
Yes, that she kiss me in the half-light, leaning
To me, and laugh and strip and stand forth in the lustre
Where lamp-light with light limb but half engages.

The flowers wax
          with buds but half perfected;
Tremble on twig that shakes when the bird strikes—
But not more fresh than she! No empery,
Though Rome and Palestine were one compact,
Would lure me from her; and with hands convening
I give me to her. But if kings could muster
In homage similar, you'd count them sages.

Mouth, now what knacks!
          What folly hath infected
Thee? Gifts, that th' Emperor of the Salonikes
Or Lord of Rome were greatly honored by,
Or Syria's lord, thou dost from me distract;
O fool I am! to hope for intervening
From Love that shields not love! Yea, it were juster
To call him mad, who 'gainst his joy engages.

ARNAUT DANIEL

Translated from Provençal by Ezra Pound

"Under the lime tree"

Under the lime tree
on the open field,
where we two had our bed,
you still can see
lovely broken
flowers and grass.
On the edge of the woods in a vale,
tandaradei,
sweetly sang the nightingale.

I came walking
to the meadow,
my love already was there.
And he received me,
Blessed Lady,
the joy of that will last.
Did he kiss me then? A thousand times, at least,
tandaradei,
look now, how my mouth is red.

Then he made
a lordly
place to lie in, all of flowers.

There's a good laugh there
even now
for anyone coming that way:
he could tell, by the roses,
tandaradei,
just where my head lay.

If anyone found out,
God forbid, he lay by me,
I'd be ashamed.
What he did with me there
may no one ever
know, except for him and me
and one little bird,
tandaradei,
which will not say a word.

WALTHER VON DER VOGELWEIDE

Translated from German by Frederick Goldin

Legends of Fatal Passion

FOR CERTAIN LOVERS in the courtly traditions, circumstances pro-duced a fate wherein mutual love was unattainable. Whether it was a married countess and her troubadour, a lover among many rivals, or lovers belonging to warring factions, the attempt to surmount the over-whelming distance between lovers often resulted in a violent and tragic ending.

❀ THE LAY OF THE TWO LOVERS
    from *The Lays of Marie de France* (c. 1160-1215?)

❀ TRISTAN AND ISOLT'S LAST DAYS
    from *Tristan and Isolt* by Gottfried von Strassburg (early
    13th century)

❀ THE LAY OF THE DOLOROUS KNIGHT
    from *The Lays of Marie de France* (c. 1160-1215?)

the lay of the two lovers

NCE UPON A TIME THERE lived amidst the Courts of Normandy two lovers, who being so completely absorbed in each other's beauty, sway of emotions, and slightest manners, they were thus brought by Love to Death. The extent of their love so dazzled the local Bretons they composed in their own tongue a song of their story, which they named the "Lay of the Two Lovers."

In Neustria—now Normandy—there was a high and great mountain where lie relics of the Two Children, whose legend was unknown. Yet these relics attracted a great deal of attention. So to accommodate the crowds of pilgrims, a king built nearby a fair and cunning city known as Pistres and named himself King of Pistres and the land, the Valley of Pistres.

Now the only daughter of this king was kind and of exquisite features, and she was very near her father's thoughts since he had lost his queen. And as the maiden gained in years, word of her beauty grew as she did in height and stature. But the king took no steps in finding her someone to wed, so that his people took him to task. So he labored hard to find a way that he might keep from facing the loss of his daughter. So he told all of those who spoke of her that she would not be wed by anyone unless he could, without rest, bear her in his arms up to the top of the great and perilous mountain.

When people heard of the king's proclamation, many young and worthy men arrived to test their strength in this quest. Yet strive as they did, the mountain and weight of the princess proved too much. Thus, for a while, no one sought this impossible task as the fallen contestants faced greater humiliation from the crowd, who were growing more impatient and hostile as the would-be husbands failed.

Now in this country lived a squire, son of a count to the king, who desired greatly to win that prize which so many before him had longed for. He had been a welcomed guest at the court for some time, and the king always enjoyed talking to him. Being a frequent guest of the court, he often spoke to the king's daughter, and as she found him handsome and kind, their intimacy with each other occurred naturally at a young age. But for fear of upsetting the matters of state, which they feared and little understood, they kept their mutual affections away from all who might pass word to their parents.

Yet the confines of their secrecy proved too small to hide their love in any longer. Their togetherness that should have provided joy began to bring also much unnecessary sorrow. It pained them endlessly that the world should be cruel toward their love. The squire sought an end to their dilemma by requesting that she elope with him so that he might avoid the impossible task of bearing her up the mountain.

"Well," said the maiden, "I know you may not carry me to the top of the mountain. However, should we elope, my father will be twice as angry and then who knows what his punishments would be. But listen to this, I have an aunt in Salerno who for more than thirty years has studied medicine. She knows everything about herbs and what they can do. Maybe you should go to her and ask her if there is an herb or medicine that will allow you to make that climb with me in your arms. My father is so powerful in this region, I can't see any other way for us."

The squire listened enthusiastically. He smiled at the cleverness of the plot for he found her craftiness appealing. So he then gathered his things and made his way by horse toward her aunt's lodgings with a small company of friends.

Once there, her aunt listened sympathetically to the young lovers' plight. She heard the story of how they met and of their desires to be with one another and how her niece's father did not wish it to be so unless he complete that extremely difficult task. She found the king's task unfair without question. So when the squire asked her to provide him with some drug that could help him carry his love up the mountain, she was very willing to give him something.

So this kind lady made a potion, and pouring it into a little flask, gave it him, saying, "No matter how worn or tired you may be, by drinking from this flask, you will feel all your bones and your heart and blood revive greatly. All you must do is drink it when the right time arrives." He was excited and thrilled that he could possess such a drink, and after thanking her many times and promising her many favors in turn, he made his way back to his lodgings.

He now felt confident enough to ask the king for his daughter's hand in marriage. The king smiled at his innocent sincerity, but then he attempted to make him realize his slight build of body, his slender arms, and his inexperience at proving himself worthy even at sports.

But as this critique by the king did not deter him from what he sought to do, so the king, unable to do anything else, set a date for the young man to make his attempt at climbing the mountain and winning his daughter.

Now as none had tried bringing her up the mountain in some time, news of the squire's bid to succeed at this daring feat revived the town's interest in this quest. So it soon became something everyone felt necessary to attend. And for the daughter's part, to aid him in his struggle, she took to fasting.

When the appointed day arrived, the young man went to the site early, bringing with him the flask with its potent drink. Soon a great crowd gathered and then the king appeared leading his daughter, who was dressed in only a plain and simple smock.

After addressing the crowd, the king bid him to lift his daughter and make his attempt up the mountain as best he could. On this note, he picked her up and proceeded at a good pace as the crowd cheered uncontrollably behind them. Soon he was halfway up the mountain and the crowd's calls of encouragement faded to only an echo of their original source. Although he now began to feel his muscles tighten, he was still continuing at a pace that pleased him. The task at hand became all consuming and he took pleasure in enduring the hardship his love caused him. He no longer felt it her father's test but a test of his own. The flask with its clever potion was there about his neck ingeniously disguised as an amulet, but he saw no need for it now. The struggle to bring her up the mountain brought him face to face with a limit of his own. And this limit, this dark unknown mask of himself he encountered, he recognized as his manhood. He was the boy facing the man whom he would be. In carrying his love, he found inside himself now a voice that encouraged him even further.

Yet for all his self-realizations, she felt him tire and his arms grow slack. She asked him and then pleaded with him to take the drink that was in the flask. But he couldn't. "My courage is wrought up," he replied. "I've come too far to rely on any unknown medicine now. It could help my limbs and muscles, yes, but I fear it would destroy something else I've gained, this joy in being able to carry you alone without crutch or vehicle."

Soon they were more than two-thirds up the mountainside, but his strength became so fragile that a young boy of eight could've pushed him over. She grew worried, and pleaded with him again.

"Please, my love, take the drink. I want to see you succeed. Please, do, do it for me—do not become so involved in this test. My father is cruel and this test is just trickery. Do not kid yourself that this is fair sport. Take the drink and let's outwit him so that I can be free of him and be always with you." And with these last words, she kissed him.

He listened, but then he grew angry that she should so break his concentration. He heard her talk but he could no longer listen. When she kissed him, he smiled all he could, but this only made him more convinced that he must carry on without the aid of her aunt's drug. The summit of the mountain was just ahead. If he needed to be focused, this was the time he needed to be focused most. He was afraid of what the drug might do to him now that he was so close. So fixing his gaze on the path and staring ahead, he continued. The summit was near at hand and approachable.

Then squeezing the last ounce of strength out of him, and with a mighty push, and then another, he at last reached the final plateau of the mountain and stepped onto its peak. But as he did so, his body collapsed and his heart burst, spilling blood from his mouth.

When the young maiden felt him fall, and saw that he could no longer move, and felt his pulse and found him dead, she cried such shrill cries of sorrow that no one had doubt of his fate. Her yells of pain became unbearable and many in the crowd turned away from the summit and sobbed, while others took action and ran up the mountain to assist the tragic couple, while others yet threatened the king with calls for his head.

The young princess continued her cries. Then upon finding the flask around his neck, she removed it and shattered its glass casing against a rock nearby. Her wails continued again, horribly. Then seeing her lover dead, she took him in her arms and, pressing him close, kissed his eyes and mouth dearly. Her sorrow was too great for her young heart, and her will craving death brought her to the brink of exhaustion. In this manner she died.

Now when the townspeople reached the summit, the entire scene saddened them greatly. Finding both of them lifeless, yet wrapped closely in each other's arms, they dared not remove the bodies from this place that cost them their lives. So they brought a fair and marvelously wrought coffin of marble to the plateau, and with the counsel of the holy men laid them softly to rest there on the mountaintop.

So they remained there forever alone, surrounded only by the many strange and wonderful flowering herbs the contents of the flask gave life to. This mountain, that had previously been re-

nowned for its mysterious image of the Two Children, now became
known throughout the Breton region and far abroad as the Mountain of the Two Lovers.

And there our story ends.

from THE LAYS OF MARIE DE FRANCE

Translated from French by Eugene Mason, adapted by the editor

tristan and isolt's last days

NOW KAHEDIN, THE BROTHER OF ISOLT, had loved
from his earliest days a fair maiden from a neighboring
land, and in turn she, too, loved him well. Yet her parents,
against her will, had given her in marriage to another knight, the
lord of Gamaroch, which lay near to the land of Arundel. And there
in his castle of Gamaroch, did her husband keep her secure within
his home, for he knew well that she loved him not; and never would
he leave his land without having her securely guarded.

Then Kahedin in his sorrow took counsel with Tristan, and Tristan told him he should, by any means, get word to his lady to tell
her to make molds in wax of the castle gate keys while her husband
slept, and then to throw the molds into the moated ditch below the
castle wall.

Thus upon hearing of Tristan's plan, she did exactly this, and
with the aid of a cunning smith they made keys that would fit the
locks.

So when next Nampotenis, for so was the knight called, rode
abroad and left his wife in guard, Kahedin and Tristan came secretly and unlocked the castle gates and entered. The lady received
them with much joy; but before entering the castle, as they crossed
the moated ditch, a sharp wind loosened the circlet from Kahedin's
helmet and it fell to the ground unnoticed by all.

Then Kahedin and his lady spoke together through the hours of the night, and Tristan kept watch without till the sun began to dawn. With the morning light they rode away and deemed that none knew of their visit.

But when Nampotenis returned to his castle in the morning, he spotted the circlet from Kahedin's helmet and, recognizing its make, reasoned it to be from him whom he knew his wife loved. So with stern words he asked her to confess the truth, and because she greatly feared his wrath and cruelty, she told him all; and Nampotenis therewith called his men together, pursued after the two knights, and overtook them in the forest.

Being unaware that they had been discovered, they were taken by surprise. Nampotenis fell on Kahedin and ran him through the body with his spear, so that he fell dead. But Tristan in wrath drew out his sword and ran upon Nampotenis and smote him dead, and put all his men to flight. Yet before they fled, one of his men pierced Tristan through the thigh with a poisoned spear. With great sorrow did Tristan bear his dead comrade back to Karke, and they buried him in the monastery.

His wife, Isolt of the White Hand, dressed Tristan's wound, and then let the leeches of the land do what they might to heal him, but so potent was the poison that their work could not overcome it.

Then Tristan saw well how it stood with him, and he said to himself, "Now might I but send for my lady, Isolt the Queen, I think she might cure me now; otherwise must I die of this hurt."

Then secretly he sent for his most trusted messenger, Kurwenal, and prayed for him to go with great speed to Tintagel and seek out Isolt the Queen.

"Bring with thee this ring, and show it to her as a token from me; and say how that I lie sorely wounded and must needs die if she come not to my aid. And if for love of me she will come, then I pray thee to set a white sail to the ship; but if she cometh not, then let the sail be black, for I shall know she loveth me no more."

Then Kurwenal departed, even as Tristan asked him to do so, and came to Tintagel, and told Isolt the Queen secretly all that Tristan had bade him say. She made ready in haste and wrapped herself in her veil. She stole to the harbor and sailed away before any might know of it.

Now Tristan asked all attending him to bring him to the shore day by day so that he might watch for the ship from Cornwall till his weakness grew so great that he could no longer go to the water's edge. Then he asked his wife, Isolt of the White Hand, to watch from the window of his chamber and bear him tidings when Kurwenal should return.

But Isolt of the White Hand had listened secretly when her husband spoke to Kurwenal, and her heart was hot within for anger against the other Isolt, for she knew of his deep love for her. So when at last she spied the ship that bore Isolt the Queen, she said to her husband, "Now cometh the ship that Kurwenal sailed from here."

"Please Isolt, telleth me, what color is the sail that the ship carries?" said Tristan.

" 'Tis black, my love, black as the darkest night," said Isolt of the White Hand, yet she lied, for the sail was white as snow.

Then Tristan spoke no more, but turned his face to the wall, and said in his heart, "God keep thee well, my love Isolt, for I shall never look on thee again." With that he loosed his hold on the thin strand that held his life and let his soul depart.

Now the ship that held Isolt of Ireland drew near the shore; and as they approached the land, she heard bells toll from the monastery and the chapels, and lamentation in the streets.

"Why this woe?" asked Isolt the Queen, "and why do you toll the bells?" Then an old man answered, and said, "Fair lady, a great misfortune has fallen over our land. Tristan, the bravest of knights, he who drove out our enemies and restored our duke to his own land, is just now dead. He died of a wound from a poisoned spear; and they have just now borne his body to the monastery."

Then Isolt said no more, but went toward the monastery swiftly; and all looked upon her, and marveled at her beauty and her woe. And when she came to the monastery, Tristan lay dead on the bier, and beside him sat Isolt of the White Hand. Then Isolt the Queen looked at her: "Why do you sit there beside the dead, thou who hast done most to slay him? Arise, and get thee gone!" And Isolt of the White Hand arose and drew aside, for she greatly feared the beautiful queen.

But Isolt of Ireland spoke no more to anyone, but laid her down on the bier by her lover; and put her arms around him and sighed once, and her soul departed from her body.

Now word reached King Mark that Isolt his queen had fled with Kurwenal. So he took ship and, pursuing her, came upon the land only to find Isolt dead beside the fallen Tristan. And then seeing the king, Kurwenal told Mark all that happened, and the secret of the love potion, and how it was by the magic of the love drink that the two had wronged him. And Mark spoke, weeping: "Aie! Tristan, had thou but trusted in me, and told me all the truth, then had I given Isolt to thee to be thy wife."

Then he bid those attending the bodies to embalm them both, and he bore them back with him to Tintagel, and laid them in marble tombs on either side of the chapel wherein the kings of his line lay buried. And by the tomb of Tristan he bid them plant a rose tree, and by that of Isolt a vine, and the two reached toward each other across the chapel, and wove branches and root so closely together that no man thereafter might separate them.

from TRISTAN AND ISOLT by Gottfried von Strassburg
Translated from German by Jessie Weston, adapted by the editor

the lay of the dolorous knight

 OW LISTEN TO A LAY I once heard a minstrel chanting to his harp. "The Lay of the Dolorous Knight," the harper called his song, but for some of those who heard it, they called it instead, "The Lay of the Four Sorrows."

In Nantes, of Brittany, there dwelt a lady who was much loved by all, for she possessed many good traits both in mind and body. So kind, fair, and intelligent was this woman, that throughout the realms nearby no knight could resist her charms, even though he saw her but only once. So great were the riches of this lady, that she was courted by the lords of her country, both night and day and in winter and summer.

Now in Brittany lived four young barons, whose names are of no matter. What is important is that they were desirable in the eyes of young maidens for their looks, wealth, and kind manners. Now each of these four knights had set his heart upon this woman and, for love of her, their hearts pained them greatly. And they did all that they could do in the manner of courtly love to gain her favors above all the rest.

On her side, the lady was perplexed and troubled and could not make a swift end to her dilemma. "Now which of these four knights should I make my friend?" she said to herself over again. For each time she counted up each of the courtier's many good points, she found the final answer so puzzling she needed to count again. Then, after rehearsing their good qualities for an umpteenth time, she declared that all four were worthy of her love, for in adding up all their good traits she found this practice so much more desirable than subtracting. So to each and all, she made herself fair and open, giving to all four her courtly favor, and they in return gave gifts and charming letters. Thus every knight thought himself above the other three, and in their messages they diligently strove more and more to please her in song and words. And in their knightly sport, they wore for her to see either some pennant, sleeve, or ring she had privately given them.

Now when Eastertide was come, a great tournament was announced to be held just outside the city walls of Nantes, a very rich city. The four lovers were called to the tourney, as well as other knights from faraway countries who rode to the games to break a lance in honor of their lady.

After the four lovers had laced their harnesses, they issued forth from the city to the tournament grounds, followed by other knights who were friends and of the same company. But it was the four lovers who were called to carry the day and enter the games first. So against the four knights, armed in coats of mail and with their shields and lances, were arrayed four other knights, two of whom were of Hainault and two of Fleming. When the four lovers saw their adversaries ready themselves for combat, and their lady looking down upon them from her chair, they had little desire to flee, but each hastened to join in battle. They lowered their spears and, choosing their enemies, met them so eagerly that no one questioned the outcome, for their enemies along with their horses fell to earth. Yet, the four lovers reckoned little of their plight so desirous were they to show their prowess to their lady that they dismounted and set upon their foes with sword and hastened them to yield for their lives. Now when the friends of the vanquished knights saw their trial, they hurried to their help, and demanded the four lovers to put an end to their deeds beyond the pale of this sport. But before they could make reply, the friends of the four lovers pressed into action and then challenged their foes. So in the din, many words were not heard, but many strong strokes of the swords were seen. Thus the games soon broke into a melee.

The damsel of the four lovers stood up to watch these feats of arms, and greatly impressed was she by their daring deeds. Yet she could not say which one did best or was most deserving of praise, so she watched intently as all four swung their swords and shields.

Now the tournament was no longer even a seemingly ordered battle. The ranks of the two companies that strove against one another were so pressed together and so mixed, their confusion caused them to turn upon their fellow. Soon so fierce grew the fighting that no one could tell whether he struck a comrade or foe. The four lovers did well and their lady prized them all, but, as the evening drew near, their courage led them to folly. Having ventured too far from their peers, they were set upon by their adversaries and attacked so fiercely that three were slain outright. For the fourth, he still lived but was completely mauled. His thigh was broken, a spearhead was trapped in his side, and his arm injured so it was now useless.

The field was filled with the bodies of those who had fallen as well as those of the four lovers. Their shields were placed under them, and their bodies then brought into the city with much honor. The whole city was moved with pity, and the mourning went on for days long and loud. A ceremony was set with each knight still living passing by the fallen with their helmets at hand, their hauberks unlaced, and their heads bent in sorrow. But the three fallen lovers, because of their wild behavior, brought contempt into many a knight's look.

With the ceremony finished, the three fallen bodies and the wounded fourth body were brought to the house of the lady who greatly loved them all. And knowing of their terrible adventure, she fell down in a swoon and mourned their fate by calling out their names, one by one.

"Aie," she said, "I shall never have four knights trust their hearts to me again. Never again shall I be so happy. For despite all their wealth, their well-mannered ways, and their handsome looks, they chose my love above all others. Poor great knights! These loyal and generous men! I couldn't choose one then, and I can't choose one now. I'm sorry for all of them. Three are dead, and the fourth wounded beyond repair. Never again will I hear their words in song. There is only one thing to do and that is give the slain their proper burial and attend to the other hopefully to heal his wounds."

So this noble and proud lady gave the three slain knights a fine burial in a rich and worthy abbey. And to the fourth she called in surgeons and doctors who healed his wounds slightly so that he might live in as little pain as possible. She continued to care for him and cherished his presence in the house, but she never forgot the other three knights and, for this reason, she went about the house in great sorrow and in lasting pity.

Sometime after the tragedy occurred, the lady and her knight were at their meals when the lady broke out crying for her sorrows that had yet to leave. The knight looked earnestly upon her. For when she lifted her head and gazed at him, he could see that this woman was very much removed from him. That she was still mourning his comrades, he had no doubt.

"My noble lady," he said, "what is it that so troubles you?"

"Dear friend," she replied, "I am thinking of what has happened and remember your friends, who are now dead. Never have I heard of a lady of my standing ever loved by four such valiant knights, nor ever lost them all in a single day. Save you—who were so maimed and so physically challenged—all are gone. Therefore I find myself the saddest lady under the sun. To remember these things, of you four I shall make a Lay, and will call it the 'Lay of the Four Sorrows.' "

When the knight heard these words, he made swift reply.

"My lady, do not call it the 'Lay of the Four Sorrows,' but, rather, the 'Lay of the Dolorous Knight.' For my three comrades have finished their course; they have nothing more to hope for in this life. They are gone, and with them the knowledge of their great love for you. I alone have survived, greatly amazed and fearful, but I find my life more bitter than my comrades must've found the grave. For I see you coming and going, and I speak with you during your matins and vespers, but no tangible joy do I receive—no embraces, no kisses, not even your hand to hold. Nothing do I get but a few empty, courteous words from you. Since all these things have come to pass because of you, I find myself waiting on death instead of life. For this reason, your Lay should bear my name, and be called the 'Lay of the Dolorous Knight.' He who would name it the 'Lay of the Four Sorrows' would name it wrongly, and not according to the truth."

Thus she thought the matter over. So once the Lay was composed and finished and knowing what pain the first title brought him, she told him she would call it the "Lay of the Dolorous Knight." Yet she still continued to sorrow at the loss of her four brave and handsome men, and so to others she called it the "Lay of the Four Sorrows," so now many know of the song by that name. In our lands, however, it is called the "Lay of the Dolorous Knight," for many deem to know the truth of the matter. Yet either title you may use as it becomes you, for here the story ends, and nothing more is to be said and nothing more do I know. *Au revoir.*

from THE LAYS OF MARIE DE FRANCE

Translated from French by Eugene Mason, adapted by the editor

the Codes of Courtly Love

ANDREAS CAPELLANUS'S Tractatus de Amore et de Amoris Re-media, *which contains* The Rules of Courtly Love *presented here, is loosely based on Ovid's* Ars Amatoria. *It reflects what the women of court desired in their knight or troubadour. Also included in this section is the wisdom of the troubadours, which shows an age as keen to fashion and appearance as our own era.*

the Rules of courtly love

1. *Marriage is no real excuse for not loving.*

2. *He who is not jealous cannot love.*

3. *No one can be bound by a double love.*

4. *It is well known that love is always increasing or decreasing.*

5. *That which a lover takes against the will of his beloved has no relish.*

6. *Boys do not love until they arrive at the age of maturity.*

7. *When one lover dies, a widowhood of two years is required of the survivor.*

8. *No one should be deprived of love without the very best of reasons.*

9. *No one can love unless he is impelled by the persuasion of love.*

10. *Love is always a stranger in the home of avarice.*

11. *It is not proper to love any woman whom one would be ashamed to marry.*

12. *A true lover does not desire to embrace in love anyone except his beloved.*

13. *When made public, love rarely endures.*

14. *The easy attainment of love makes it of little value; difficulty of attainment makes it prized.*

15. *Every lover regularly turns pale in the presence of his beloved.*

16. *When a lover suddenly catches sight of his beloved, his heart palpitates.*

17. *A new love puts to flight an old one.*

18. *Good character alone makes any man worthy of love.*

19. *If love diminishes, it quickly fails and rarely revives.*

20. *A man in love is always apprehensive.*

21. *Real jealousy always increases the feeling of love.*

22. *Jealousy, and therefore love, are increased when one suspects his beloved.*

23. *He whom the thought of love vexes eats and sleeps very little.*

24. *Every act of a lover ends in the thought of his beloved.*

25. *A true lover considers nothing good except what he thinks will please his beloved.*

26. *Love can deny nothing to love.*

27. *A lover can never have enough of the solaces of his beloved.*

28. *A slight presumption causes a lover to suspect his beloved.*

29. *A man who is vexed by too much passion usually does not love.*

30. *A true lover is constantly and without intermission possessed by the thought of his beloved.*

31. *Nothing forbids one woman being loved by two men or one man by two women.*

from THE ART OF COURTLY LOVE by Andreas Capellanus

Translated from French by J. J. Parry

"So through the eyes love attains the heart"

So through the eyes love attains the heart,
Because of the heart are the eyes the Turkmans,
And the eyes go to reconnoitre,
This that it shall please the heart to retain.
And when they are well agreed,
And firm all three in the same resolve
True love then takes birth,
From this that the eyes make agreeable to the heart;

And wanting this, it can neither be born, nor have
    commencement.
By the grace and by the command
Of the three, and by their pleasure
Is born love, that with good hope
Goes his friends comforting;
Because all accomplished lovers
Know that love is perfect benevolence.
That it is born of the heart and of the eyes, is without doubt;
And the eyes cause to flower and the heart to fructify
Love, that is the fruit of their very seed.

GIRAUT DE BORNELH

Translated from Provençal by John Rutherford

codes and maxims of noble conduct

FOR THE YOUNG PAGE OR SQUIRE

 HUN THE COMPANIONSHIP of fools, impertinents, or meddlers, lest you pass for the same. Never indulge in buffoonery, scandal, deceit, or falsehood. Be frank, generous, and brave; be obliging; study neatness in your dress and let elegance of fashion make up for plainness of material. Never allow a seam to remain ripped and gaping; it is worse than a rent: the first shows ill-breeding; the last only poverty, which is by far the lesser evil of the two. There is no great merit in dressing well if you have the means; but a display of neatness and taste on a small income is a sure token of superiority of spirit. You must have a mistress; that is essential to your position as a gentleman; but be true to her, and make no boast of her favors. To perfect your manners, you must to the court: that is the true seminary of politeness. There weak minds are strengthened and strong minds perfected. If you take service, let it be with a man of worth and liberality. Study to please him without bending to his worse qualities. Show no jealousy of those around him; distribute his favors and his bounty as he pleases. Have your arms, et cetera, always ready for use. Be first up in the morning, and, when called upon, first also in the saddle. In the tourney, do not fail to display all your dexterity and valor.

AMANIEU DES ESCAS

FOR THE COURTIER

BE ALWAYS NEAT and elegant in your dress, no matter what the material. See that your linen be fine and white and that your shoes, stockings, doublet, & et cetera, be well fitting, so that everyone may admire them. Let your gown, if you wear one, be rather short than long. Let your mantle be of the same stuff as your gown, and let the girdle and clasp be properly arranged. A gentleman should be particularly careful of his hair. It should be frequently washed, and it is better to wear it short than long. Be careful how you carry your hands and use your eyes; do not stare rudely, nor let your fingers dangle or move about awkwardly.

ARNAUD DE MARSANS

FOR THE KNIGHT

BE ALWAYS WELL MOUNTED. Let a charger, swift of foot and easy to manage, be always led in your train. Your arms should be costly and well kept, and your shield, lance, and curass of good proof. Look well to the trapping of your horse. The saddle and crupper should be of the same color; so should your shield and the streamer of your lance. Have a horse to carry your baggage; thus you will never be taken at a short, but always be found ready for war or tilt—always ready to take advantage of an opportunity for gaining honor and renown, and for recommending yourself to the ladies. In war be ever vigilant. Make it a point of honor to be foremost in the onset, and last in the retreat. At the tournament be provided with several spears and helms. Have your horse garnished with bells; the sound inspirits the animal and his rider and terrifies his foe. Never return from the lists without an encounter. When your lance fails you, draw your sword and strike till the clatter startles hell and heaven!

ARNAUD DE MARSANS

ADVICE TO A COUNT

COUNT OF TOULOUSE, if you wish to be prized: be loyal, liberal, and magnificent; bestow splendid gifts on friends and strangers; be always ready to give and always reluctant to refuse; persecute your enemies and favor your friends.

GUY OF CAVAILLON

TO FRIENDS

I LOVE GOOD FRIENDS, good cheer, and handsome presents. I hate parsimony, a friend who fails me in the day of need, the man who speaks evil of dice, and the sorry fellow who refuses to play.

MONK OF MONTAUDUN

FOR THE CAVALIER

A LOYAL GENTLEMAN who loves a lady whom he fears and respects would be guilty of great wrong were he to allow himself to die in silence of his passion. It is his duty to explain his feelings to the lady of his choice before allowing himself to come to such an extremity. I advise you, therefore, to make known your affection, and to request your lady to retain you as her cavalier. If she be prudent and courteous she will not take it amiss. Far from considering your request dishonoring, she will esteem you the more for it. Indeed, such, is your worth that there is not a lady in the world, even

were she a queen or an empress, that ought not to consider herself
happy in having such an one for her knight.

BEATRICE, LADY OF MONTFERRAT

A MISCELLANY OF APHORISMS

THE BASE SOUL is careless of renown.

GUILHEM D'AGOULT

IT IS A REPROACH and a shame to change one's mind lightly.

NAT DE MONS

I REGRET THE PENNIES of my friend are not all gold coins, since
he is just the man to enrich those who suffer from the rapacity of
others.

RAIMOND DE DURFORT

EMBRACE LOVE WHILE it is offered. Seize the happy moment; it
is a flower that quickly fades.

PEYRE D'AUVERGNE

AT LEAST, BEAUTIFUL LADY, whatever torment I endure, it will
still be glorious to hope; for a rich and noble hope is better than a
worthless gift.

AYMERIE OF BEAUVOIR

I REVIVE WITH THE SPRING, which reanimates all nature, and
pours into my soul the soft effusions of love.

PEIRE VIDAL

from THE TROUBADOURS by John Rutherford

At the Courts of Love

THE DOMINANT FORM of poetry in this section, the tenzon *allowed for two poets to propose and dispute a single subject or question. Their lyrics not only projected their own personal view, but allowed the listener—through the tempo of the poet's verse—to gather the intent of their heart. The subject matter of these* tenzons *gives the reader an idea of a "question of love" that a petitioner might have presented at a Court of Love.*

※ *Tenzon*

> Alamanda (late 12th century) and Giraut de Bornelh (d. after 1211)

※ *Tenzon*

> Isabella (born c. 1180) and Elias Cairel (late 12th century)

※ Of Beauty and Duty

> Dante Alighieri (1265-1321)

Tenzon

Alamanda and Giraut de Bornelh

f I seek your advice, pretty friend Alamanda,
don't make things hard for me, for I'm a banished man.
For that's what your deceitful mistress told me,
that now I've been expelled from her command:
and what she gave me she retracts now and reclaims.
What should I do?
I'm so angry that my body's
all but bursting into flame.

In God's name, Giraut, a lover's wishes
count for nothing here, for if one partner fails
the other should keep up appearances
so that their trouble doesn't spread or grow.
If she tells you that a high peak is a plain,
believe her,
and accept the good *and* bad she sends:
thus shall you be loved.

I can't keep from speaking out against her pride,
even if you're young and beautiful and blond.
The slightest pain hurts me, the smallest joy overwhelms,
and still I'm not in first or second place.
I'm worried that this anger will destroy me:
you praise me,
but I can tell—I'm closer to the waves
and I think you're leading me astray.

If you come to me with questions so profound,
my God, Giraut, I don't know what to say.
You call to me with a joyful, easy heart,
but I want to mow my field before someone else tries;

if I wanted to arrange a peace
I would have looked for you,
but since she keeps her lovely body hidden so,
I think you're right that you've been ditched.

Now don't start yakking, young girl,
for she lied to me first, more than five times.
Do you think I can put up with this much more?
I'd be taken for an ignoramus.
I have a mind to ask about another friendship
if you don't shut up;
I got much better counsel from Na Berengeira
than I ever got from you.

Now I see, Giraut, that she's capable of everything,
since you call her fickle and unfaithful;
still, do you think she wants to patch things up?
I doubt she's that tame yet:
from now on she'll keep courtesy in last place,
no matter what you say.
She's so angry with you that she'll suffer
neither peace nor oath nor treaty.

Beauty, for God's sake, don't let me lose your aid—
you already know how it was granted me.
If I've done wrong in being so irate,
don't hold it against me; and if you've ever felt how fast
a lover's heart can change, or if you've ever loved,
think of some way;
for I'm as good as dead if I have lost her—
but don't tell her that.

Seigneur Giraut, I didn't want your love to end,
but she says she has a right to be enraged,
because you're courting someone else in front of everyone
who next to her's worth nothing, clothed or nude.

If she didn't jilt you she'd be acting weak,
since you're courting someone else.
But I'll speak well of you to her—I always have—
if you promise not to keep on doing that.

Beauty, for God's sake, if she has your trust,
promise her for me.

I'll gladly do so, but when she's given you her love again,
don't take yours back.

ALAMANDA AND GIRAUT DE BORNELH

Translated from Provençal by Meg Bogin

Tenzon

Isabella and Elias Cairel

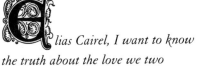 *lias Cairel, I want to know*
the truth about the love we two
once had; so tell me, please,
why you've given it to someone else.
For your song doesn't sound the way it did,
and I never held myself back from you,
nor did you once demand such love from me
but that I wasn't instantly at your command.

My lady Isabella, in those days
you showed dignity
and joy and strength and wit and wisdom,
but if I sang your praises

it wasn't out of love
but for the profit I might get from it,
just as any joglar sings a lady's fame:
but you kept changing every day.

Elias Cairel, I've never seen
a lover who would trade
his lady's love for riches,
and if I were to speak against him,
I've so often praised him no one would believe me.
Go ahead, double your insanity:
as for me, I'm much improved,
although for you I have no use.

Lady, I'd be crazy to remain
another day in your domain;
still, I don't despair
just because I don't have fame and profit;
you will stay the way the people want you,
and I'll go pay a visit to my pretty friend
whose body's graceful and well-kept,
whose heart is neither lying nor deceitful.

Elias Cairel, you're a phoney
if I ever saw one,
like a man who says he's sick
when he hasn't got the slightest pain.
If you'd listen, I'd give you good advice:
go back to your cloister,
and don't dare pronounce my name again
except in prayer to the patriarch Ivan.

Lady Isabella, in a monks' refectory
I've never taken morn nor evening meal,
but you'll have ample opportunity

for your fresh color will soon fade.
Against my will you make me say cruel things,
and I have lied: for there's no woman
worthier than you, nor one more beautiful
in the whole world; that's why I suffer.

If you don't mind, Elias,
I'd like to know who your new lady is:
so tell me, and don't be afraid,
that I may judge her worth and her intelligence.

Lady, what you ask would be a foolish thing;
I don't want to risk her friendship,
and I'm scared the *lauzengiers* will talk:
therefore I don't dare speak my desire.

ISABELLA AND ELIAS CAIREL
Translated from Provençal by Meg Bogin

Of Beauty and Duty

wo ladies to the summit of my mind
    Have clomb, to hold an argument of love.
    The one has wisdom with her from above,
For every noblest virtue well designed:
The other, beauty's tempting power refined
    And the high charm of perfect grace approve:
    And I, as my sweet Master's will doth move,
At feet of both their favours am reclined.
Beauty and Duty in my soul keep strife,
    At question if the heart such course can take

And 'twixt two ladies hold its love complete.
The fount of gentle speech yields answer meet,
That Beauty may be loved for gladness' sake,
And Duty in the lofty ends of life.

DANTE ALIGHIERI

Translated from Italian by Dante Gabriel Rossetti